D1490703

THE SEASONABLE ANGLER

THE
SEASONABLE
ANGLER

Nick Lyons

Atlantic Monthly Press
New York

Copyright © 1970 by Nick Lyons

All rights reserved. No part of this book may be reproduced in any form or by any electronic or mechanical means, including information storage and retrieval systems, without permission in writing from the publisher, except by a reviewer, who may quote brief passages in a review. Any members of educational institutions wishing to photocopy part or all of the work for classroom use, or publishers who would like to obtain permission to include the work in an anthology, should send their inquiries to Grove/Atlantic, Inc., 841 Broadway, New York, NY 10003.

Published simultaneously in Canada
Printed in the United States of America

A section of Chapter 1 originally appeared in slightly different form, in *Field & Stream* (February 1969) under the title "First Trout, First Lie." Chapter 5, "Mecca," appeared in *Field & Stream* (November 1968). These stories copyright © 1968, 1969 by *Field & Stream*.

A section of Chapter 2 originally appeared, in somewhat different form, in *Sportfishing* (April 1969) under the title "Opening Day Madness." copyright © 1969 by *Sportfishing* Magazine.

The poem "Trouting" appeared in *The New York Times* (July 7, 1966) under the title "The Trout." Copyright © 1966 by The New York Times Company. Reprinted by permission.

Library of Congress Cataloging-in-Publication Data

Lyons, Nick.
    The seasonable angler / Nick Lyons.
        p.   cm.
    Originally published: New York : Funk & Wagnalls, 1970.
    ISBN 0-87113-744-5
    1. Fishing. I. Title.
SH441.L95   1999
799.1'757—dc21   98-45975

Atlantic Monthly Press
841 Broadway
New York, NY 10003

99 00 01 02   10 9 8 7 6 5 4 3 2 1

For Mari

"Is it not an art to deceive a trout with an artificial fly? a trout! that is more sharp-sighted than any hawk you have named and more watchful and timorous than your high-mettled merlin is bold!"

"a generous fish . . . he also has seasons."

—Izaak Walton

Contents

Preface

There is a rhythm to the angler's life and a rhythm to his year.

If, as Father Walton says, "angling is somewhat like poetry, men are to be born so," then most anglers, like myself, will have begun at an age before memory—with stout cord, bamboo pole, long, level leader, bait hook, and worm. Others, who come to it late, often have the sensation of having found a deep and abiding love, there all the while, like fire in the straw, that required only the proper wind to fan it forth. So it is with a talent, a genius even, for music, painting, writing; so it is, especially, with trout fishing—which "may be said to be so like the Mathematics that it can never be fully learnt."

There is, or should be, a rhythmic evolution to the fisherman's life (there is so little rhythm today in so many lives). At first glance it may seem merely that from barefoot boy with garden hackle to fly-fisherman with all the delicious paraphernalia that makes trout fishing a consummate ritual, an enticing and inexhaustible mystery, a perpetual delight. But the evolution runs deeper, and incorporates at least at one level an increasing respect for the "event" of fishing (I would not even call it "sport") and of nature, and a diminishing of much necessary interest in the fat creel.

But while the man evolves—and it is the trouter, quite as much as the trout, that concerns me— each year has its own rhythm. The season begins in the dark brooding of winter, brightened by innumerable memories and preparatory tasks; it bursts out with raw action in April, rough-hewn and chill; it is filled with infinite variety and constant expectation and change throughout midspring; in June it reaches its rich culmination in the ecstatic major hatches; in summer it is sparer, more demanding, more leisurely, more philosophic; and in autumn, the season of "mellow fruitfulness," it is ripe and fulfilled.

And then it all begins again. And again.

I am a lover of angling, an *aficionado*—even an addict. My experiences on the streams have been intense and varied, and they have been compounded by the countless times I have relived them in my imagination. Like most fishermen, I have an abnormal imagination—or, more bluntly, I have been known to lie in my teeth. Perhaps it comes "with the territory." Though I have been rigorous with myself in this book, some parts of it may still seem unbelievable. Believe them. By now I do. And why quibble? For this is man's play, angling, and as the world becomes more and more desperate, I further respect its values as a tonic and as an antidote—on the stream and in the imagination—and as a virtue in itself.

These then are the confessions of an angling addict—an addict with a "rage for order," a penchant for stretchers, and a quiet desire to allow the seasons to live through him and to instruct him.

TROUTING

Laying it out long, the yellow line,
with delicate fly
plumply perched upon its hackles high,
I can with most strategic efforts probe
opaquest corners of this stream—
riffled, pocketed, baggy, deep—
where denizens quick and mottled lie,
shadows in the shimmering glass,
a dream wherein our starkest portions dance:
then with a crash the shadow streaks
out of the dark, and cracks the dream:
and there's the fish, wet and struggling
on the end—silver, sleek, and cold—
that has me in its desperate hold.

THE SEASONABLE ANGLER

1/Winter Dreams and Wakening

*"The gods do not deduct from man's
allotted span the hours spent in fishing."*
—BABYLONIAN PROVERB

When do I angle?
Always.

Angling is always in season for me. In all
seasons I fish or think fish; each season
makes its unique contribution, and there is no
season of the year when I am not angling. If indeed the gods do not deduct, then surely I will be
a Struldbrug.

Yet sometimes in October I do not think angling. The lawful season has recently ended, I
have neglected my far too numerous affairs grossly,
my four children have begun school and are already cutting up, my wife trots out her winter
repair list. It is a busy, mindless time.

But it is good that my secret trouting life lie fallow—after one season, before another. I welcome the rest. Sometimes this period in October lasts as long as seven or even eight days.

But by late October, never later than the twenty-third or twenty-fourth, the new season commences—humbly perhaps, but then there it is.

Perhaps the office calendar will inaugurate the new year this year. Casually I may, on a blustery late-October afternoon, notice that there are only sixty-eight days left to the year: which means, since the next is not a leap year, that there are exactly one hundred and fifty-eight days left until Opening Day. I have long since tabulated the exact ninety days from January first until April first. It is not the sort of fact one forgets.

Or a catalog may arrive from one of the scores of sporting houses that have me on their lists. I leave it on the corner of my desk for a day, two days, a full business week, and then one lunch hour chance to ruffle through its pages, looking at the fine bamboo rods with hallowed names like Orvis, Pezon et Michel, Payne, the Hardy and Farlow reels, the latest promises in fly lines, the interminable lists of flies, the sporting clothes.

Yes, perhaps this year I shall buy me a Pezon et Michel instead of that tweedy suit my wife assures me I need, or a pair of russet suede brogues with cleated heels and fine felt soles.

In my mind I buy the rod and receive it in the long oblong wooden box, unhouse it for the first time, flex it carefully in my living room. Then I am on the Willowemoc or the West Branch and I thread the line and affix the fly and the line is sailing out behind me and then looping frontward, and then it lies down softly and leader-straight on the gin-clear water, inches from the steadily opening circles of a good brown steadily rising.

Yes, there is every reason why I should buy a Pezon et Michel this year. And a pair of brogues.

Or perhaps one evening after I have lit the fire, my wife may be talking wisely about one of the supreme themes of art, love, shopping, or politics, and she will notice that I am not there.

"You're not at all interested in what I have to say about Baroque interiors," she says.

"Yes. You know I am, Mari. I couldn't be more interested."

"You didn't hear a word I said."

I frown. "Frankly, I was thinking of something else. Something rather important, as a matter of fact."

My wife looks at me for a long time. She is an artist, finely trained and acutely sensitive to appear-

ances. Then she says, with benign solicitude—
for herself or me, I cannot tell—"But it's only October."

"My mind drifted," I say.

"Not the Beaverkill! *Already?*"

"No. To be absolutely truthful, I was not on
the Beaverkill."

"The West Branch of the Croydon? Fishing
with Horse Coachmen?"

"Croton. Hair Coachman. Actually," (I mum-
ble) "actually, I was on the Schoharie, and it was
the time of the Hendricksons, and . . ."

And then she knows and I know and soon all
my four children—who know everything—know,
and then the fever smokes, ignites, and begins to
flame forth with frightening intensity.

I take every piece of equipment I own from
my fishing closets. I unhouse and then wipe down
my wispy Thomas and my sturdy old Granger
carefully. I check each guide for rust. I look for
nicks in the finish. I line up the sections and note
a slight set in the Thomas, which perhaps I can
hang out by attaching to it one of my children's
blocks and suspending them from the shower rod.
(My children watch—amused or frightened.) I
rub dirt out of the reel seat of the Thomas. I

take apart my Hardy reel and oil it lightly. I toss out frayed and rotted tippet spools. I sit with my Granger for a half hour and think of the fifteen-inch brown I took with it on the Amawalk, with a marabou streamer fished deep into a riffled pool the previous April.

From the bedroom my wife calls. I grumble unintelligibly and she calls again, winsomely. I grumble again and continue my work: I steel-wool the male ferrule of my Thomas and whistle into its mate.

Then I dump all the hundreds and hundreds of my flies into a shoe box, all of them, and begin plucking them out one by one and checking for rust or bent wings or bruised tails; I hone points, weed out defectives, relacquer a few frayed head knots, and then place the survivors into new containers. I have numberless plastic boxes and metal boxes and aluminum boxes—some tiny, some vest-pocket size, some huge storage boxes. Each year I arrange my flies differently, seeking the best logic for their placement. Is the Coachman more valuable next to the Adams? Will I use the Quill Gordon more next year? Should all the midge flies go together? Only three Hendricksons left. Strange. I'll have to tie up a dozen. And some

Red Quills. And four more #16 Hairwing Coachmen. And perhaps that parachute fly, in case I make the Battenkill with Frank.

There is very little genuine custom in the world today, and this is a consummate ritual: the feel of a Payne rod, its difference in firm backbone from a Leonard or a parabolic Pezon et Michel; the feel of a particular felt or tweed hat; those suede brogues with cleated heels and fine felt soles; the magic words, "Beaverkill," "Willowemoc," "Au Sable," "Big Bend," and "trout" itself; the tying and the repairing; the familiar technical talk, the stories. Fishing is not for wealthy men but for dreamers.

Have I always had so serious a case? Practically. That is the safest answer I can give. Practically. I cannot remember a time when I was not tinkering with my equipment; I cannot remember a time when I did not think about fishing.

And each item of tackle is charged with memories, which return each winter in triumphant clarity out of the opaque past: a particular fly recalls a matched hatch on the translucent Little Beaverkill near Lew Beach; a nick in my Thomas recalls a disastrous Fathers' Day weekend evening on the East Branch when I almost lost the rod and forfeited my married life. And the mangled handle on my Hardy reel summons that nightmarish fire that raged in on the crest of furious winds during the dead of winter, buffaloing up out of the stone church next door and doing its work quick and voracious as a fox on a chicken raid.

I remember the policeman's light flicking through my little study. My fly-tying table—with all the hooks and hackles, threads and bobbins—had been decimated. I had raced to the closet, its door seared through. With the borrowed flashlight I searched into the hollowed-out section of the wall. My vest, in which I had most of my working tackle, hung loosely from a wire hanger. It was almost burned away. On one side, several plastic boxes had been chewed through: the flies were all singed or destroyed; nothing could be saved there. Little items—like tippet spools, leader sink, fly dope, clippers, penlite, and extra leaders—could be replaced easily enough: they were all gone. My waders were a lump of melted rubber; my old wicker creel was a small black skeleton on a rear nail; an ancient felt hat was a mere bit of rag; several glass rods without cases had gone up; a fine old net that had always been there at the crucial moments was only a charred curved stick; and a whole shelf of storied angling knick-knacks had collapsed and lost itself in the wet, black debris on the floor. In a corner, the aluminum rod cases were roasted black (Frank Mele later got Jim Payne to check them out: they are no doubt the better for it). And in the debris I found the Hardy reel, its chamois case burned away, the fine floating line devoured, the plastic handle mutilated.

And every carlisle hook I ever see—long and impractical—recalls my first trout, my first fishing lie.

My first angling experiences were in the lake that bordered the property my grandfather owned when the Laurel House in Haines Falls, New York, was his. At first no one gave me instruction or encouragement, I had no fishing buddies, and most adults in my world only attempted to dissuade me: they could only be considered the enemy.

It was a small, heavily padded lake, little larger than a pond, and it contained only perch, shiners, punkinseeds, and pickerel. No bass. No trout. Invariably I fished with a long cane pole, cork bobber, string or length of gut, and snelled hook. Worms were my standby, though after a huge pickerel swiped at a small shiner I was diddling with, I used shiners for bait also, and caught a good number of reputable pickerel. One went a full four pounds and nearly caused my Aunt Blanche to leap into the lake when, after a momentous tug, it flopped near her feet; she was wearing open sandals. She screeched and I leaped toward her—to protect my fish.

I also caught pickerel as they lay still in the quiet water below the dam and spillway. It was not beneath me to use devious methods; I was in those days cunning and resourceful and would lean far over the concrete dam to snare the pickerel with piano-wire loops. It took keen discipline to lower the wire at the end of a broomstick or willow sapling, down into the water behind the sticklike fish, slip it abruptly (or with impeccable slowness) forward to the gills, and yank.

After the water spilled over at the dam it formed several pools in which I sometimes caught small perch, and then it meandered through swamp and woods until it met a clear spring creek; together they formed a rather sizeable stream, which washed over the famous Kaaterskill Falls behind the Laurel House and down into the awesome cleft.

Often I would hunt for crayfish, frogs, and newts, in one or another of the sections of the creek—and use them for such delightful purposes as frightening the deliciously frightenable little girls, some of whom were blood (if not spiritual) relations.

One summer a comedian who later achieved some reputation as a double-talker elicited my aid in supplying him with small frogs and crayfish; it was the custom to have the cups turned down at the table settings in the huge dining room, and he would place my little creatures under the cups of those who would react most noticeably. They did. Chiefly, though, I released what I caught in a day or so, taking my best pleasure in the catching itself, in cupping my hand down quickly on a small stream frog, grasping a bull frog firmly around its plump midsection, or trapping the elusive back-dancers as they scuttered from under upturned rocks in the creek bed.

Barefoot in the creek, I often saw small brightly colored fish no more than four inches long, darting here and there. Their spots—bright red and gold and purple—and their soft bodies intrigued me, but they were too difficult to catch and too small to be worth my time.

That is, until I saw the big one under the log in the long pool beneath a neglected wooden bridge far back in the woods. From his shape and coloration, the fish seemed to be of the same species, and was easily sixteen or seventeen inches long. It was my eighth summer, and that fish completely changed my life.

In August of that summer, one of the guests at the hotel was a trout fisherman named Dr. Hertz. He was a bald, burly, jovial man, well over six-foot-three, with knee-cap difficulties that kept him from traveling very far by foot without severe pains. He was quite obviously an enthusiast: he had a whole car-trunk-full of fly-fishing gear and was, of course, immediately referred to me, the resident expert on matters piscatorial.

But he was an adult, so we at once had an incident between us: he refused, absolutely refused, to believe I had taken a four-pound pickerel from "that duck pond," and when he did acknowledge the catch, his attitude was condescending, unconvinced.

I bristled. Wasn't my word unimpeachable? Had I ever lied about what I caught? What reason would I have to lie?

Yet there was no evidence, since the cooks had dispatched the monster—and could not speak English. Nor could I find anyone at the hotel to verify the catch authoritatively. Aunt Blanche, when I recalled that catching to her in Dr. Hertz's presence, only groaned "Ughhh!"—and thus lost my respect forever.

Bass there might be in that padded pond, the knowledgeable man assured me: pickerel, never.

So we wasted a full week while I first supplied him with innumerable crayfish and he then fished them for bass. Naturally, he didn't even catch a punkinseed.

But it was the stream—in which there were obviously no fish at all—that most intrigued him, and he frequently hobbled down to a convenient spot behind the hotel and scanned the water for long moments. "No reason why there shouldn't be trout in it, boy," he'd say. "Water's like flowing crystal and there's good stream life. See. See those flies coming off the water."

I had to admit that, Yes I did see little bugs coming off the water, but they probably bit like the devil and were too tiny to use for bait anyway. How could you get them on the hook? About the presence of trout—whatever they might be—I was not convinced.

And I told him so.

But old Dr. Hertz got out his long bamboo rod, his delicate equipment, and tried tiny feathered flies that floated and tiny flies that sank in the deep convenient pools where the creek gathered before rushing over the falls and down into the cleft.

Naturally, he caught nothing.

He never even got a nibble—or a look, or a

flash. I was not surprised. If there *were* trout in the creek, or anywhere for that matter, worms were the only logical bait. And I told him so. Worms and shiners were the only baits that would take *any* fish, I firmly announced, and shiners had their limitations.

But I did genuinely enjoy going with him, standing by his left side as he cast his long yellow line gracefully back and forth until he dropped a fly noiselessly upon the deep clear pools and then twitched it back and forth or let it rest motionless, perched high and proud. If you could actually catch fish, any fish, this way, I could see its advantages. And the man unquestionably had his skill—though I had not seen him catch a fish, even a sunny, in more than a week.

And that mattered.

As for me, I regularly rose a good deal earlier than even the cooks and slipped down to the lake for a little fishing by the shore. I had never been able to persuade the boat-boy, who did not fish, to leave a boat unchained for me; unquestionably, though he was only fourteen, he had already capitulated to the adults and their narrow, unimaginative morality. One morning in the middle of Dr. Hertz's second, and last, week, I grew bored with the few sunfish and shiners and midget perch available from the dock and followed the creek down through the woods until I came to the little wooden bridge.

I lay on it, stretching myself out full length, feeling the rough weathered boards scrape against my belly and thighs, and peered down into the clear water.

A few tiny dace flittered here and there. I spied a small bull frog squatting in the mud and rushes on the far left bank—and decided it was not worth my time to take him. Several pebbles slipped through the boards and plunked loudly into the pool. A kingfisher twitted in some nearby oak branches, and another swept low along the stream's alley and seemed to catch some unseen insect in flight. A small punkinseed zig-zagged across my sight. Several tiny whirling bugs spun and danced around the surface of the water. The shadows wavered, auburn and dark, along the sandy bottom of the creek; I watched my own shimmering shadow among them.

And then I saw him.

Or rather, saw just his nose. For the fish was resting, absolutely still, beneath the log-bottom brace of the bridge, with only a trifle more than his rounded snout showing. It was not a punkinseed or a pickerel;

shiners would not remain so quiet; it was scarcely a large perch.

And then I saw all of him, for he emerged all at once from beneath the log, moved with long swift gestures—not the streak of the pickerel or the zig-zag of the sunfish—and rose to the surface right below my head, no more than two feet below me, breaking the water in a neat little dimple, turning so I could see him, massy, brilliantly colored, sleek and long. And then he returned to beneath the log.

It all happened in a moment: but I knew.

Something dramatic, miraculous, had occurred, and I still feel a quickening of my heart when I conjure up the scene. There was a strong nobility about his movements, a swift surety, a sense of purpose—even of intelligence. Here was a quarry worthy of all a young boy's skill and ingenuity. Here, clearly, was the fish Dr. Hertz pursued with all his elaborate equipment. And I knew that, no matter what, I had to take that trout.

I debated for several hours whether to tell Dr. Hertz about the fish and finally decided that, since I had discovered him, he should be mine. All that day he lay beneath a log in my mind, while I tried to find some way out of certain unpleasant chores, certain social obligations like entertaining a visiting nephew my age—who simply hated the water. In desperation, I took him to my huge compost pile under the back porch and frightened the living devil out of him with some huge night crawlers—for which I was sent to my room. At dinner I learned that Dr. Hertz had gone off shopping and then to a movie with his wife; good thing, I suppose, for I would surely have spilled it all that evening.

That night I prepared my simple equipment, chose a dozen of my best worms from the compost pile, and tried to sleep.

I could not.

Over and over the massive trout rose in my mind, turned, and returned to beneath the log. I must have stayed awake so long that, out of tiredness, I got up late the next morning—about six.

I slipped quickly out of the deathly still hotel, too preoccupied to nod even to my friend the night clerk, and half ran through the woods to the old wooden bridge.

He was still there! He was still in the same spot beneath the log!

First I went directly upstream of the bridge and floated a worm down to him six or seven times.

Not a budge. Not a look. Was it possible?

I had expected to take him, without fail, on the

first drift—which would have been the case were he a perch or huge punkinseed—and then march proudly back to the Laurel House in time to display my prize to Dr. Hertz at breakfast.

I paused and surveyed the situation. Surely trout must eat worms, I speculated. And the morning is always the best time to fish. Something must be wrong with the way the bait is coming to him. That was it.

I drifted the worm down again and noted with satisfaction that it dangled a full four or five inches above his head. Not daring to get closer, I tried casting across stream and allowing the worm to swing around in front of him; but this still did not drop the bait sufficiently. Then I tried letting it drift past him, so that I could suddenly lower the bamboo pole and provide slack line and thus force the worm to drop near him. This almost worked, but, standing on my tip toes, I could see that it was still too high.

Sinkers? Perhaps *that* was the answer.

I rummaged around in my pockets, and then turned them out onto a flat rock: penknife, dirty handkerchief, two dried worms, extra snelled hooks wrapped in cellophane, two wine-bottle corks, eleven cents, a couple of keys, two rubber bands, dirt, a crayfish's paw—but no sinkers, not even a washer or a nut or a screw. I hadn't used split shot in a full month, not since I had discovered that a freely drifting worm would do much better in the lake and would get quite deep enough in its own sweet time if you had patience.

Which I was long on.

I scoured the shore for a tiny pebble or flat rock and came up with several promising bits of slate; but I could not, with my trembling fingers, adequately fashion them to stay tied to the line. And by now I was sorely hungry, so I decided to get some split shot in town and come back later. That old trout would still be there. He had not budged in all the time I'd fished over him.

I tried for that trout each of the remaining days that week. I fished for him early in the morning and during the afternoon and immediately after supper. I fished for him right up until dark, and twice frightened my parents by returning to the hotel about nine-thirty. I did not tell them about the trout, either.

Would they understand?

And the old monster? He was always there, always beneath the log except for one or two of those sure yet leisurely sweeps to the surface of the crystal stream, haunting, tantalizing.

I brooded about whether to tell Dr. Hertz after

all and let him have a go at my trout with his fancy paraphernalia. But it had become a private challenge of wits between that trout and me. He was not like the huge pickerel that haunted the channels between the pads in the lake. Those I would have been glad to share. This was my fish: he was not in the public domain. And anyway, I reasoned, old Dr. Hertz could not possibly walk through the tangled, pathless woods with his bum legs.

On Sunday, the day Dr. Hertz was to leave, I rose especially early—before light had broken—packed every last bit of equipment I owned into a canvas bag, and trekked quickly through the wet woods to the familiar wooden bridge. As I had done each morning that week, I first crept out along the bridge, hearing only the sprinkling of several pebbles that fell between the boards down into the creek, and the twitting of the stream birds, and the bass horn of the bull frog. Water had stopped coming over the dam at the lake the day before, and I noticed that the stream level had dropped a full six inches. A few dace dimpled the surface, and a few small sunfish meandered here and there.

The trout was still beneath the log.

I tried for him in all the usual ways—upstream, downstream, and from high above him on the bridge. I had by now, with the help of the split shot, managed to get my worm within a millimeter of his nose, regularly; in fact, I several times that morning actually bumped his rounded snout with my worm. The old trout did not seem to mind. He would sort of nudge it away, or ignore it, or shift his position deftly. Clearly he considered me no threat. It was humbling, humiliating.

I worked exceptionally hard for about three hours, missed breakfast, and kept fishing on into late morning on a growling stomach. I even tried floating grasshoppers down to the fish, and then a newt, even a little sunfish I caught upstream, several dace I trapped, and finally a crayfish.

Nothing would budge that confounded monster.

At last I went back to my little canvas pack and began to gather my scattered equipment. I was beaten. And I was starved. I'd tell Dr. Hertz about the fish and if he felt up to it he could try for him.

Despondently, I shoved my gear back into the pack.

And then it happened!

I pricked my finger sorely with a huge carlisle hook, snelled, which I used for the largest pickerel. I sat down on a rock and looked at it for a moment, pressing the blood out to avoid infection, washing my finger in the spring-cold stream, and then wrapping it with a bit of shirt I tore off—which I'd get hell for. But who cared.

The carlisle hook! Perhaps, I thought. Perhaps.

I had more than once thought of snaring that trout with piano wire lowered from the bridge, but too little of his nose was exposed. It simply would not have worked.

But the carlisle hook!

Carefully I tied the snelled hook directly onto the end of my ten-foot bamboo pole, leaving about two inches of firm gut trailing from the end. I pulled it to make sure it was firmly attached, found that it wasn't, and wrapped a few more feet of gut around the end of the pole to secure it.

Then, taking the pole in my right hand, I lay on my belly and began to crawl with painful slowness along the bottom logs of the bridge so that I would eventually pass directly above the trout. It took a full ten minutes. Then, finally, there I was, no more than a foot from the nose of my quarry, directly over him.

I scrutinized him closely for a long moment, lowering my head until my nose twitched the surface of the low water but a few inches from his nose.

He did not move.

I did not move.

I watched the gills dilate slowly; I followed the length of him as far back beneath the log as I could; I could have counted his speckles. And I trembled.

Then I began to lower the end of the rod slowly, slowly, slowly into the water, slightly upstream, moving the long bare carlisle hook closer and closer to his nose.

The trout opened and closed its mouth just a trifle every few seconds.

Now the hook was fractions of an inch from its mouth. Should I jerk hard? Try for the under lip? No, it might slip away—and there would be only one chance.

Instead, I meticulously slipped the bare hook directly toward the slight slit that was his mouth, guiding it down, into, and behind the curve of his lip.

He did not budge. I did not breathe.

And then I jerked abruptly up!

The fish lurched. I yanked. The bamboo rod splintered but held. The trout flipped up out of his element and into mine and flopped against the buttresses of the bridge. I pounced on him with both hands, and it was all over. It had taken no more than a few seconds.

Back at the hotel I headed immediately for Dr.

Hertz's room, the seventeen-inch trout casually hanging from a forked stick in my right hand. To my immense disappointment, he had gone.

I wrote to him that very afternoon, lying in my teeth.

> Dear Doctor Hertz:
>
> I caught a great big trout on a worm this morning and brought it to your room but you had gone home already. I have put into this letter a diagram of the fish that I drew. I caught him on a worm.

I *could* have caught him on a worm, eventually, and anyway I wanted to rub it in that he'd nearly wasted two weeks of my time and would never catch anything on those feathers. It would be a valuable lesson for him.

Several days later I received the letter below, which I found some months ago in one of my three closets crammed with fly boxes, waders, fly-tying tools and materials, delicate fly-rods, and the rest of that equipment needed for an art no less exhaustible than the "Mathematics."

> Dear Nicky:
>
> I am glad you caught a big trout. But after fishing that creek for a whole two weeks I am

convinced that there just weren't any trout in it. Are you sure it wasn't a perch? Your amusing picture looked like it. I wish you'd sent me a photograph instead, so I could be sure. Perhaps next year we can fish a *real* trout stream together.

Your friend,

THOS. HERTZ, M.D.

Real? Was that unnamed creek not the realest I have ever fished? And *"your friend."* How could he say that?

But let him doubt: I had, by hook and by crook, caught my first trout.

And when I have dreamed that first trout a thousand times, it is time to think of the present. For the new year has turned. A new start has been made. A new President has been inaugurated. Has he heard C. L. Sulzberger's words? "Perhaps it is a source of weakness in American foreign policy that so few of its chief architects, our Presidents and Secretaries of State, have been anglers and therefore endowed with the necessary skill and philosophical temperament required in statesmanship."

And how many more, presidents and secretaries of their own estates, could not profit from angling?

I mark their interior policy mark'd on their faces, their words, their gait: the rebel with too little stillness; the conservative with too little adventure left in his bones; the pedant whose mind could be brushed with the rush of a clear mountain stream; the desperate man whose heart might be cheered and quickened by the sudden rise of a trout; the vain artist who rides the latest fad who might be humbled by the lawful awesomeness of nature; the businessman busy at getting and spending who might there gain greater profits; the bored man who could marvel in the infinite variety of the stream and the lay of the trout and the innumerable permutations and combinations necessary to bring the strike.

But I grow moralistic and slip into pride, the greatest of the seven deadlies—the hubris that trouting should also still.

Then, inside me, the spring trout begin to stir: I feel them deep in their thawing streams—lethargic, slow. I begin to feel the coverts gouged out of the stream floors, the tangled roots and waterlogged branches, the whitened riffles and soft sod banks. Yes, the year has turned. And has not Frank written me: "There are forty-three days left until the season opens, Nick—and you had better give some serious thought to your tying." And he encloses a spritely barred rock neck and, on the spot, I tie up three Spent-wing Adamses.

And then it is time to lay down Schwiebert and Jennings, to set aside Halford and Marinaro, to put up my Walton with those well-underlined passages. I begin to frequent the tackle stores during lunch hour; I stop off at Abercrombie's on my way to work to flex a Payne rod (for what day is not blessed by having first flexed a Payne); I write out an elaborate order to Orvis—but realize it is far beyond my means and whittle it down; a bit of wood duck, an impala tail, floss, assorted necks, two spools of fine silk thread arrive from the economical Herter's. And then, in the evenings—all the tugs and tightenings of the day dissolved—I sit down at my vise and begin to tie.

In my salad days, February and March were filled with action. To wet an early line, I would travel to Steeplechase pier at Coney Island and stand, near-frozen, with other hardy souls on a windy day casting lead and spearing down for ugly hackleheads, skates, and miniature porgies. Later I would practice fly casting on the snow— or in gymnasiums. And as March grew I would wade the tidal flats for winter flounder and that strange grab bag of the seas found at the Long Island shore.

But now I am older and can wait less anxiously. Sometimes. I try to remember that the season will come in its own good time. It cannot be rushed.

My hands are busy at the vise; I use the back of a match to seal and varnish a last guide or two; I send for travel folders I cannot afford to use; I remember a huge trout rising in a small unnamed creek, a little boy slipping a bare carlisle hook up into its mouth—and then, with a momentous yank, the new season has begun.

2/The Lure of
Opening Day

"*Who so that first to mille comth, first grynt.*"
—GEOFFREY CHAUCER,
Prologue to "The Wife of Bath's Tale"

The whole madness of Opening Day fever is quite beyond me: it deserves the complexities of a Jung or a Kafka, for it is archetypal and rampant with ambiguity. And still you would not have it.

Is it simply the beginning of a new season, after months of winter dreams?

That it is *one* day—like a special parade, with clowns and trumpets—that is bound by short time, unpredictable weather, habit, ritual?

That it is some massive endurance test?

Or the fact that the usually overfished streams are as virgin as they'll ever be?

That there are big fish astream—for you have caught your largest on this day?

Masochism—pure and simple?

A submergence syndrome?

That you are the first of the year—or hope to be? And will "first grynt"?

I don't know. I simply cannot explain it. When I am wise and strong enough (or bludgeoned enough), I know I shall resist even thinking of it.

I know for sure only that March is the cruelest month—for trout fishermen. And that the weakest succumb, while even the strongest must consciously avoid the pernicious lure of Opening Day.

On approximately March fourth, give or take a day—I get up from my desk year after year and industriously slip into the reference room, where I spend hours busily studying the *Encyclopaedia Britannica*, Volume I, under "Angling": looking at pictures of fat brook trout being taken from the Nipigon River, impossible Atlantic salmon bent heavy in a ghillie's net, reading about Halford and Skues and the immaculate Gordon and some fool in Macedonia who perhaps started it all.

Then on lunch hours I'll head like a rainbow trout, upstream, to the Angler's Cove or the Roost or the ninth floor at Abercrombie's—sidle up to groups rehashing trips to the Miramachi, the

Dennys, the Madison, the Au Sable, the Beaverkill, and "this lovely little river filled with nothing
less than two-pounders, and everyone of 'em
dupes for a number twenty-six Rube Winger."

It is hell.

I listen intently, unobtrusively, as each trout
is caught, make allowances for the inescapable
fancy, and then spend the rest of the day at my
desk scheming for this year's trips and doodling
new fly patterns on manuscripts I am supposed to
be editing. Or some days I'll head downstream,
and study the long counter of luscious flies under
glass at the elegant William Mills', hunting for
new patterns to tie during the last March flurry of
vise activity.

It is a vice—all of it: the dreaming, the reading
(Aston to Zern), the talking, the scant hours (in
proportion to all else) of fishing itself. How many
days in March I try to get a decent afternoon's
work done, only to be plagued, bruited and
beaten, by images of browns rising steadily to
Light Cahills on the Amawalk, manic Green
Drake hatches on the big Beaverkill, with dozens
of fat fish sharking down the ample duns in slow
water. I fish a dozen remembered streams, two
dozen from my reading, a dozen times each, every
riffle and eddy and run and rip and pool of them,

every March in my mind. I become quite convinced that I am going mad. Downright berserk.
Fantasy becomes reality. I will be reading at my
desk and my body will suddenly stiffen, lurch
back from the strike; I will see, actually see, four,
five, six trout rolling and flouncing under the alder
branch near my dictionary, glutting on leafrollers
—or a long dark shadow under a far ledge of
books, emerging, dimpling the surface, returning
to its feeding post.

My desk does not help. I have it filled with
every conceivable aid to such fantasies. *Matching the Hatch*, Art Flick's *Streamside Guide, The
Dry Fly and Fast Water* reside safely behind brown
paper covers—always available. There are six or
seven catalogs of fly-fishing equipment—from
Orvis and Norm Thompson and Dan Bailey and
Herter's and Mills; travel folders from Maine,
Idaho, Quebec, Colorado—all with unmention-
able photos of gigantic trout and salmon on them;
I have four Sulfur Duns that Jim Mulligan
dropped off on a visit—that I *could* bring home;
and there is even a small box of #16 Mustad dry-
fly hooks and some yellow-green wool, from
which I can tie up a few heretical leafrollers peri-
odically, hooking the barb into a soft part of the
end of the desk, and working rapidly, furtively, so

no one will catch me and think me quite so trout-sick mad as I am.

But no. It is no good. I will not make it this year. I cannot wait until mid-May, when even then there will be difficulty abandoning Mari and my children (still under trouting size) for even a day's outing.

And yet for many years there was this dilemma: after years of deadly worming and spinning, I became for a time a rabid purist, shunning even streamers and wet flies. How could I fish Opening Day with dries? It was ludicrous. It was nearly fatal.

But it was not always so.

I can remember vividly my first Opening Day, and I can remember, individually, each of the ten that succeeded it, once at the expense of the College Entrance examinations, once when I went AWOL from Fort Dix, and once . . . well . . . when I was in love.

A worm dangled from a nine-foot steel telescopic rod took my second trout. He was only a stocked brown of about nine inches, and I took him after three hours of fishing below the Brewster bridge of the East Branch of the Croton; I was just thirteen and it was the height of the summer.

On Opening Days you can always see pictures

THE LURE OF OPENING DAY

of the spot in the New York papers. Draped men, like manikins, pose near the falls upstream; and Joe X of 54-32 Seventy-third Avenue is standing proudly with his four mummy buddies, displaying his fat sixteen-inch holdover brown, the prize of the day; a buddy has ten—are they smelt? You do not die of loneliness on the East Branch of the Croton these days.

Probably it was always like that. But memory is maverick: the crowds are not what I remember about the East Branch—not, certainly, what I remember about my first day.

In the five years since I had caught my first trout, I had fished often for large-mouth bass, pickerel, perch, sunfish, catfish, crappies, and even shiners—always with live bait, usually with worms, always in lakes or ponds. Once, when my mother tried to interest me in horseback riding, I paused at a creek along the trail, dismounted, and spent an hour fishing with a pocket rig I always carried.

It could not have been the nine-inch hollow- and gray-bellied brown that intrigued me all that winter. Perhaps it was the moving water of the stream, the heightened complexity of this kind of fishing. Perhaps it was the great mystery of moving water. What does Hesse's Siddhartha see in the river? "He saw that the water continually flowed and flowed and yet it was always there; it was always the same and yet every moment it was new." He saw, I suppose, men, and ages, and civilizations, and the natural processes.

Whatever the cause, the stream hooked me, too. All that winter I planned for my first Opening Day. There were periodic trips to the tackle stores on Nassau Street, near my father's office; interminable lists of necessary equipment; constant and thorough study of all the outdoor magazines, which I would pounce on the day they reached the stands.

My parents were out of town the weekend the season was to open, and my old grandmother was staying with me. My plan was to make the five forty-five milk train out of Grand Central and arrive in Brewster, alone, about eight. My trip had been approved.

I arose, scarcely having slept, at two-thirty by the alarm and went directly to the cellar, where all my gear had been carefully laid out. For a full ten days.

I had my steel fly rod neatly tied in its canvas case, a hundred and fifty worms (so that I would not be caught short), seventy-five #10 Eagle

Claw hooks (for the same reason), two jackknives (in case I lost one), an extra spool of level fly line, two sweaters (to go with the sweat shirt, sweater, and woolen shirt I already wore under my Mackinaw), a rain cape, four cans of Heinz pork and beans, a whole box of kitchen matches in a rubber bag (one of the sporting magazines had recommended this), a small frying pan, a large frying pan, a spoon, three forks, three extra pairs of woolen socks, two pairs of underwear, three extra T-shirts, an article from one of the magazines on "Early Season Angling" (which I had plucked from my burgeoning files), two tin cups, a bottle of Coca-Cola, a pair of corduroy trousers, a stringer, about a pound and a half of split shot, seven hand-tied leaders, my bait-casting reel, my fly reel, and nine slices of rye bread. Since I had brought them down to the cellar several days earlier, the rye bread was stale.

All of this went (as I knew it would, since I had packed four times, for practice) into my upper pack. To it I attached a slightly smaller, lower pack, into which I had already put my hip boots, two cans of Sterno, two pairs of shoes, and a gigantic thermos of hot chocolate (by then cold).

Once the two packs were fastened tightly, I

tied my rod across the top (so that my hands would be free), flopped my felt hat down hard on my head, and began to mount my cross.

Unfortunately, my arms would not bend sufficiently beneath the Mackinaw, the sweater, the woolen shirt, and the sweat shirt—I had not planned on this—and I could not get my left arm through the arm-strap.

My old grandmother had risen to see me off with a good hot breakfast, and, hearing me moan and struggle, came down to be of help.

She was of enormous help.

She got behind me, right down on the floor, on my instructions, in the dimly lit basement at three in the morning, and pushed up. I pushed down.

After a few moments I could feel the canvas strap.

"Just a little further, Grandma," I said. "Uhhhh. A . . . litt . . . ul . . . more."

She pushed and pushed, groaning now nearly as loudly as I was, and then I said, "NOW!" quite loudly and the good old lady leaped and pushed up with all her might and I pushed down and my fingers were inside the strap and in another moment the momentous double pack was on my back.

I looked thankfully at my grandmother standing

(with her huge breasts half out of her nightgown) beneath the hanging light bulb. She looked bushed. After a short round of congratulations, I told her to go up the narrow stairs first. Wisely she advised otherwise, and I began the ascent. But after two steps I remembered that I hadn't taken my creel, which happened to contain three apples, two bananas, my toothbrush, a half pound of raisins, and two newly made salami sandwiches.

Since it would be a trifle difficult to turn around, and I was too much out of breath to talk, I simply motioned to her to hand me the creel from the table. She did so, and I laboriously strapped it around my body, running the straps, with Grandma's help, under the pack.

Then I took a step. And then another. I could not take the third. My steel fly rod, flanged out at the sides, had gotten wedged into the narrow stairwell. In fact, since I had moved upstairs with some determination, it was jammed tightly between the two-by-four banister and the bottom of the ceiling.

It was a terrifying moment. I *could* be there all day. For weeks.

And then I'd miss Opening Day.

Which I'd planned all that winter.

I pulled. Grandma pushed. We got nowhere. But

[37]

then, in her wisdom, she found the solution: re-move the rod. She soon did so, and I promptly sailed up the stairs at one a minute.

A few moments later I was at the door. "I'll . . . have . . . to hurry," I panted. "It's three thirty-five . . . already."

She nodded and patted me on the hump. As I trudged out into the icy night I heard her say, "Such a pack! Such a little man!"

The walk to the subway was only seventeen blocks, and I made it despite that lower pack smacking painfully at each step against my rump. I dared not get out of my packs in the subway, so I stood all the way to Grand Central, in near-empty cars, glared at by two bums, one high-school couple returning from a dress dance, and several early workers who appeared to have seen worse.

The five forty-five milk train left on time, and I was on it. I unhitched my packs (which I did not —could not—replace all that long day, and thus carried by hand), and tried to sleep. But I could not: I never sleep before I fish.

The train arrived at eight, and I went directly to the flooding East Branch and rigged up. It was cold as a witch's nose, and the line kept freezing at the guides. I'd suck out the ice, cast twice, and find ice caked at the guides again. After a few moments at a pool, I'd pick up all my gear, cradling it in my arms, and push on for another likely spot.

Four hours later I had still not gotten my first nibble.

Then a sleety sort of rain began, which slowly penetrated through all my many layers of clothing right to the marrow-bone.

But by four o'clock my luck had begun to change. For one good thing, I had managed to lose my lower pack and thus, after a few frantic moments of searching, realized that I was much less weighted down. For another, it had stopped raining and the temperature had risen to slightly above freezing. And finally, I had reached a little feeder creek and had begun to catch fish steadily. One, then another, and then two more in quick succession.

They weren't trout, but a plump greenish fish that I could not identify. They certainly weren't yellow perch or the grayish large-mouth bass I had caught. But they were about twelve to fourteen inches long and gave quite an account of themselves after they took my night crawler and the red and white bobber bounced under water.

They stripped line from my fly reel, jumped two or three times, and would not be brought to net without an impressive struggle.

Could they be green perch?

Whatever they were, I was quite pleased with myself and had strung four of them onto my stringer and just lofted out another night crawler when a genial man with green trousers and short green jacket approached.

"How're you doin', son?" he asked.

"Very well," I said, without turning around. I didn't want to miss that bobber going under.

"Trout?"

"Nope. Not sure what they are. Are there green perch in this stream?"

"Green perch?"

Just then the bobber went under abruptly and I struck back and was into another fine fish. I played him with particular care for my audience and in a few moments brought him, belly up, to the net.

The gentleman in back of me had stepped close. "Better release him right in the water, son; won't hurt him that way."

"I guess I'll keep this one, too," I said, raising the fish high in the net. It was a beautiful fish—all shining green and fat and still flopping in the black meshes of the net. I was thrilled. Especially since I'd had an audience.

"Better return him now," the man said, a bit more firmly. "Bass season doesn't start until July first."

"Bass?"

"Yep. You've got a nice small-mouth there. They come up this creek every spring to spawn. Did'ya say you'd caught some more?"

I knew the bass season didn't start until July. Anybody with half a brain knew that. So when the man in green said it was a bass I disengaged the hook quickly and slipped the fish carefully back into the water.

"I'm a warden, son," the man said. "Did you say you'd caught s'more of these bass?"

"Yes," I said, beginning to shake. It was still very cold and the sun had begun to drop. "Four."

"Kill them?" he asked sternly.

"They're on my stringer," I said, and proceeded to walk the few yards upstream to where the four fish, threaded through the gills, were fanning the cold water slowly.

"Certainly hope those fish aren't dead," said the warden.

I did not take the stringer out of the icy water but, with all the grace and sensitivity I could possibly muster, and with shaking hands, began to slip the fish off and into the current. The first floated out and immediately began to swim off slowly; so did the other two—each a bit more slowly. The fourth had been on the stringer for about fifteen minutes. I had my doubts. Carefully I slipped the cord through his gills and pushed him out, too.

He floated downstream, belly up, for a few moments.

"Hmmm," murmured the warden.

"His tail moved; I'm sure it did," I said.

"Don't think this one will make it."

Together we walked downstream, following the fish intently. Every now and then it would turn ever so slowly, fan its tail, and flop back belly up again.

There was no hope.

Down the current it floated, feeble, mangled by an outright poacher, a near goner. When it reached the end of the feeder creek and was about to enter the main water, it swirled listlessly in a small eddy, tangled in the reeds, and was absolutely still for a long moment. Absolutely still.

But then it made a momentous effort, taking its will from my will perhaps, and its green back was up and it was wriggling and its green back stayed up and I nearly jumped ten feet with joy.

"Guess he'll make it," said the warden.

"Guess so," I said, matter-of-factly.

"Don't take any more of those green perch now, will you?" he said, poker-faced, as he turned and walked back up the hill. "And get a good identification book!"

I breathed heavily, smiled sheepishly, and realized that my feet were almost frozen solid. So I began to fold in my rod, gather together my various remaining goods—almost all unused—and prepare to leave. I cradled my pack in my arms and trudged up the hill to the railway station, glad I'd taken some fish, glad the fish had lived.

It was ten o'clock that night when I returned. Somehow I stumbled up the stairs and, with a brave whistle, kissed my grandmother on the cheek. She did not look like she would survive the shock of me. Then, without a word, I collapsed.

Though I had 104° fever the next day and missed a full week of school, my first Opening Day had scarcely been a failure. I had seen a few trout caught and marked where and how they had been caught. In particular, I had seen a new kind of rod and reel, the spinning outfit, which could do everything I had wanted to do with my fly rod but could not. I had seen it take trout on a small spinner fifty feet across stream from beneath an upturned tree stump—a fine fourteen-inch brown that slashed across and downstream furiously. With the trees coming directly to the water's edge, I had simply not known how to fish that fishy section with a fly rod. I had been confined, so far as I could tell, to the pools and the runs along my own bank.

That spring I worked afternoons for a gardener and soon earned enough to purchase a spinning rod of my own. I bought the longest, thinnest glass rod I could find, a Mitchel reel, and several hundred yards of braided line (monofilament had not yet appeared). I practiced with it constantly and soon, without instruction, learned to keep the rubber practice plug low and soft and accurate. I practiced underhand, side-arm, and overhand—and did not bother to fiddle with fancy bow-and-arrow or trick casts.

That summer I found my first two angling companions, Clyde and Mort, at camp, and all that fall and winter we plotted my second Opening Day with all the strategies of master generals.

This time it was not a disaster.

For us.

It *was* for the trout.

Clyde rapped on my bedroom window promptly at four o'clock, I picked up my new efficient single pack quickly, and we met Mort at Grand Central in time for the milk train.

All the way to Brewster we talked and planned, and when we arrived we marched to the stream like the four gunmen coming into town after Gary Cooper in *High Noon*. Only it was eight o'clock and freezing, and we got what we had come for.

Our spinning weapons worked with uncanny skill. By ten, Mort and I had two good trout each; Clyde had four. We picked up another seven among us before we left that afternoon and came back proud and triumphant.

Rarely after that year did we return with less than limits—often interspersed with fifteen- and sixteen-inch holdover browns. Clyde had discovered a large turn in the stream that opened into a huge deep pool with a shallow glide at its tail; midway through it a large fallen tree cut the flow and provided highly productive eddies in front and below. We dubbed it the "Big Bend" (and also named a dozen other favorite spots), and it was there that we began each Opening Day for the next half-dozen years, lined up in a row, horsing them in. The fires of each spread to the others, and we pursued unnumbered trout to their doom.

In March we'd hunt night crawlers together with flashlights on Brooklyn lawns, perfecting our technique so that we could grab low and soft and then ease the long wigglers carefully from their holes without breaking them. We'd meet annually for the Sportsmen's Show, an increasingly sordid affair; we'd send arcane messages back and forth, with code signals like TMR after EBCR—BB, OD; and we'd study carefully how to economize the tackle we carried, until we were honed instruments with no more than two dozen Eagle Claw hooks, two dozen crawlers each, a dozen of our favorite lures, and our lethal spinning gear.

Each year until we were seventeen, we'd take that five forty-five milk train out of Grand Central together, arrive at eight, and head directly through town to the Big Bend and haul 'em in. The years after, since the season officially opened at midnight, we'd arrive at eleven-thirty for brutal all-night jaunts in the icy cold. Often in those days we'd all take limits early, before the sun was fully up, and then later stretch out in the mid-morning sun for several hours before hitching home—weary and beat and proud. There are pictures of us heavily overdressed, with packs like humps on our backs; the number and size of our dead trout are as impressive as the pictures in the travel folders—or fish-shop windows. Our expressions are always absurdly inflated—or absurdly nonchalant.

It was a savage time, and we did our best to butcher that stream with our spinning rods and our night crawlers and our Homa Reversos and our C. P. Swings. We perfected our spinning so that we could bounce our lures off the tips of rocks, lay them in a one-foot pocket near a tree stump, and then flirt them back temptingly, weaving them in and out of the current, against it, into eddies, making it hang still and fluttering in the current or cruise deep. We learned how to fish our worms deep and very slow, into deep pockets and under jutting banks and fallen trees; when to fish upstream or down; where—and we knew this with uncanny skill—the trout would be lying. We learned, on that and other hard-fished streams, how to take fish when other creels were empty; we pooled our skills and knowledge and experience and became a lethal band. We learned everything except how to release a trout.

The massacre continued well into our college days, when I roomed with Mort. One year, when the season opened at six, we had decided for various reasons to cut out Clyde (who, as I shall later explain, had a few unique peculiarities on the stream). We'd driven in from Philadelphia and on up to Brewster, arriving at five and taking a large breakfast at the diner. At five-thirty, in order to beat the now mounting crowds that had found our East Branch, we headed downstream to the Big Bend.

The mists were still on the water and we felt all the old excitement sweep away the confusions of college. It was still dark and cold and no one had arrived yet as we stepped swiftly through the stark trees toward the Big Bend. As it came into view, we both felt charged with anticipation; we looked at each other and smiled.

But there was someone there before us! Up to his chest, half-hidden in the mists—and fast to a good trout! And there was someone nearby, leaping up and down.

It was Clyde—jumping the gun. And on the bank was his girl friend—a very beautiful girl friend. He heard our approach and half turned, without taking his eye from the struggling fish. Since we'd outrightly lied to him about not making it this year, we expected a bitter moment, but Clyde simply shouted, "Don't stand there! Bring the net. Quick!"

Later, when a warden saw him in the water, fast to his third pre-season trout—while we were standing glumly and honestly by—he simply lay his rod down on the bank, held up his hands, and let the trout roam about until six on a slack line.

After I began to fish with flies, I avoided Opening Day for a good number of years. I'd fish flies in their season and reckon my own opening toward late April, frequenting the fly-only stretches with their fine native populations and returning virtually all fish I took. But my family—who love me so much they scarcely can bear to part with me for a day's angling and rejuvenation of the soul—became particularly insidious in noting that I brought home no trout, and unreasonably skeptical about my having released this sixteen-incher, that two-pounder. My children began to ask those goading questions that challenge your role as a father, your very existence as an honest man.

"If you're not going to bring anything home, why go in the first place?" my wife would ask. For a painter, she has incredibly limited vision about what really matters.

So five or six years ago, when the fever was particularly severe, when I could not wait until late April, I determined to strike out boldly. I would fish Opening Day again, rid myself of the dread fever and bring home a full limit of hatchery trout. Someone else would if I didn't. I would fish with my son Paul's spinning rod. With worms. I was that desperate.

What were a few hatchery trout in comparison to my sanity? And, I calculated, a full creel on Opening Day would mean a tacit endorsement for further fishing, with flies, later in the season. And hadn't there been something challenging, raw, massy, about those long nights on the second Saturday in April? Two full-time indoor jobs, too little fishing for too long, too much absorption in the purist's craft—how can I explain my regression? I called Mort, who had not yet graduated to flies and with whom I hadn't fished in years.

"Sure," he said. "When do we leave?"

"We fish all night. Open the season at midnight . . ."

"Are you mad?" asked Mari.

". . . at the East Branch. Like the old days. I'm after meat."

"Lois!" he called. "I'm going up with Nick on Friday night. The old way."

That simple! I had brooded for two weeks, schemed with the cunning of a poacher or an adulterer, to arrange my trip. Wormers and spinners are direct, tough as Fiberglas: flies, bamboo, Keats, and a Ph.D. had made me soft.

Well, it was arranged. I was careful not to tell any of my fly-fisher friends, covertly bought two dozen #8 Eagle Claw hooks and three packets of large split shot and three dozen night crawlers in stores where I was not known as a fanatic purist, and, stowing the worms in the vegetable section of the refrigerator (to Mari's horror), began remembering those coarser, meaty days of my teens.

And then there we were, zipping along Route 22 at eleven-thirty on March thirty-first in Mort's huge Chrysler wagon. The night was nipping cold, though clear; all the old feeling was there. But now I was trimly efficient—with minimal gear, maximum comfort. It would be a killing.

"A perfect night," Mort said.

"I can remember some old ones."

"Oh, the line will freeze at the guides a bit, but we'll take 'em."

"Remember the night Clyde took three before the season opened?" We both laughed. "A man of no conscience. And that girl!"

"Good fisherman, though. Clyde was resourceful."

"Mean toward trout."

"He'd probably be poaching right now if the

New York State Conservation Department hadn't banned him from the streams. A menace——"

"I heard they paid him to leave New York every year on March fifteenth—for three months."

"It would be cheap at that price."

Mort slowed the car as we passed the Big Bend. My heart whacked against my chest. "Did you see that?" I asked, startled.

"Were they rising to midges?"

"It's a flood. Never saw it so high. And the tree is gone, the one that divided it and made those two fine eddies."

"You've been fly-fishing too long: that's been gone for six years."

"It's discolored, too."

"Never made any difference fifteen years ago," Mort said.

"Are we really *that* old? Has it been that long?"

Mort parked the car near the bridge and we watched four or five other anglers readying their gear in the glow of headlights or gas lamps.

"We'd better hurry," I advised. "My fingers are trembling." All the old raw anticipation had begun again, as it always had in my teens. We were going to make a night of it!

"I brought a furniture blanket in case we want to sack out a little later," Mort said—hopefully?

"I'm going all the way."

"Maybe."

It was colder than we'd thought, below freezing, but we rigged quickly, divided the noble worms, and headed directly downstream through the stark black trees. The moon was slightly more than a pale-yellow sliver, but our flashlights led us swiftly toward the scene of so many Opening Day slaughters.

No one was there. Not even Clyde.

The Big Bend was indeed high. The water went some ten yards higher upon the land than I had remembered it, and a close look with my flashlight showed the churning water to be thickly brownish, filled with leaves and other debris—snow water. But all the old feeling was there. I stepped out boldly up to my waist, then a bit further. The cold shot through my Totes and a small streak of icy wetness began to seep through above my knees and down into my boots. I worked myself slowly to the spot where I remembered the old fallen tree had been, the one that jutted out and cut the flow. Late one spring night we had watched browns actually leaping and snapping up insects

[53]

from its budding branches. It had been a remarkable sight. Clyde had gone mad.

Mort went slightly downstream. I could hear him crashing through the tangled hedges.

I hooked a fat night crawler several times through the neckband and cast it slightly across and upstream. In a second it had shot down past me; the flashlight showed it bobbing to the surface.

"The water's fast!" I shouted.

"And cold and dirty!" Mort shouted back. "You'd better take off that number eighteen Lady Beaverkill—she'll freeze—and put on a well-dressed Coachman, dry."

"You corrupter of purists!" I shouted. "Ironist! Wormer! Meat-Mort!"

"Maybe a number-twenty Black Gnat would bring 'em up, purist."

In another ten casts I had found a stretch of slack water. I concentrated on it, snagging my line once on the bottom, reassuringly, breaking off, and rigging up again—no small trick in the dark. But there were no nibbles. My legs began to go numb. Abruptly an image of my good wife standing at the door, shaking her head slightly as she watched me lug out my equipment, and saying, with a painfully ironic smile, "Have fun!", shot into my mind.

Well, I was having fun. It was cold as an ice cube and the stream was impossibly high and my head was beginning to throb (could you get frostbite of the head?) and my nose to run—but I felt fit and content, one with the rushing water and the stillness, out of the city, challenging nature. I lit up a cigar and cast again. It was good to be opening the season again. And how could we miss? Wasn't this the East Branch, the Big Bend, and Opening Night? Hadn't it always, without fail, produced? Wasn't this an old specialty of mine, an abused mastery—night crawlers with a spinning rod? And didn't I, to save face, have to bring home a mess of fat trout? For the honor of a father, for the fly-fishing in June?

"Got one!" Mort shouted.

"Any size?"

"Might be. Can't tell. The current's strong."

"Need the net?"

"He's big—*whoa*—he's a real old socker. Quick! Bring the net. He's huge—I can't hold him—he's heading out into the fast current. *Ya-hoooo!*"

Action! So it *was* going to be just like the old

[55]

days. I scurried ashore and up through the brush.
The beam of my light showed Mort's rod bent
sharply. I hurried faster. My Totes caught in
the brush and I felt them rip. No matter. I
dropped my rod in the bushes, got tangled in my
confounded line, freed myself, and scrambled
faster.

"*Where's that net?*"

"Coming. Coming! Big brown?"

"Must be. Haven't seen him yet—but he's big.
Damned big!"

I survived the undergrowth and came up just in
time to see the big fish spank the surface somewhat
downstream. He was genuinely huge—that much
was obvious. It was an heroic tussle, like the old
days, one of us hooked up, the other peering into
the dark, standing by happy as ghillie. The rod
would bend, the frosted gossamer line would arch
high and out across the stream. Line would be
given, line would be taken back. Soon the big
brown would slow and fumble, turn yellow belly
up, and be led gingerly toward the outstretched
net in the near dark. Flashlights would spray the
darkness, icy water would splash up my arm to the
elbow—and I would lift the net high, brandish-
ing the noble prize. Would it go twenty inches?
Would it be the largest we'd ever taken? Would its

stomach, lumpy and pink, give some clue as to what its brothers were eating? Oh, this was going to be a night! We were going to have a time of it! Just like the old days. Oh, noble sport! Oh, Olympian trout! Oh, fly-fishing in June!

"Something's wrong," Mort said flatly.

"Still got him on?"

"Yeah." Then silence. "In the tail."

"A *brown?*"

Before he could answer, I saw it was not. It was a huge mucus-colored carp, about five pounds—foul-hooked behind the dorsal fin.

"Sorry, Nick."

"Well, you get one here, you get a big one."

"Felt like a trout."

"You've been catching too many of those piker bluefish, too many stripers and lesser fare. You've forgotten, man, what a *real* fish feels like."

"Humor is one thing, purist, but don't knock the blue. *There's* a fish. Stock this ditch with blues and then you'd really have some action."

"Do they eat Sulfur Duns?"

"They eat trout and trout fisherman, purist."

"Curious," I said, beginning to trudge back through the brush, "that a blue fisherman should mistake a carp for a trout." My flashlight discovered my rod imbedded in some heavy undergrowth and I pushed my way through to it. "Very curious, indeed."

Now it was really cold. The icy water shot through the tear in my Totes and began to fill up my left leg, soon virtually dead-cold. After another dozen casts Mort sheepishly asked if I might possibly want some coffee.

I leaped out of the water.

We stopped at the bridge, where none of the twenty shivering anglers had caught even a ten-inch carp, though someone had heard of someone or other who allegedly had caught (or was it *seen?*) a seven-inch brookie.

"Did they stock the stream?" Mort asked a bundle of clothes perched on one of the bridge's bulwarks like a gargoyle.

"May not have, buddy. Snow put 'em off. Maybe up the Sodom section, but prob'ly not here. Stream's in worst shape I've seen it in over twenty-fi' years."

After coffee, during which time Mort assured me that the gargoyle must have been lying in his teeth (because if they *had* stocked the Sodom section, why was he draped over the bridge?), we headed up Route 22. Why? Mort claimed to have taken six good fish out of a certain little stream four years earlier. For this good reason we scrunched through a frozen swampy field at two-thirty, for about a half mile in. My hands were stiff and numb as we marched around under the thin light of the moon for three quarters of an hour, plunking out night crawlers here and there, never sure we were actually in water, never sure we weren't fishing in part of the flooded field. My lips trembled, my legs ached, I lost four rigs, and couldn't find a match to light up another cigar. At least my wife couldn't see me.

Finally, I simply shoved my hands deep into my pockets and began to watch Mort. If anyone can get 'em, I figured, Mort can. He's tenacious and canny and once, years ago, caught "six good fish" in this creek. Once he got one, I'd just horn in and start fishing too.

About three-thirty he hooked another good one, and after a brisk battle brought in two pounds of green weeds. They measured exactly twenty-six inches.

"Well," I said, "at least I didn't hear you call that one a trout. Might have been a bluefish—bet you thought so—but you'd never mistake even a two-pound green weed for a trout. Not even you."

Mort fished for another fifteen minutes and then we headed, not reluctantly, back through the field.

The stalks of weed, high and stiff, were frozen solid. The ground was covered with a film of delicate ice. The stars were bright. The whole universe was majestically asleep. My toes and nose were senseless.

"I mean, is it really worth it?" asked Mort.

"We're going to kill 'em," I said.

"If we're not killed first."

I was anxious, for some idiotic reason, to get back into the water at Brewster, but sadly agreed to sack out for several hours in the back of Mort's wagon. Quite obviously he was chicken—and I didn't want to embarrass him.

But I couldn't sleep.

The car was cold and hard, the big furniture blanket grimy, and I kept popping my head up to see if anyone on the bridge was catching fish. No one was. The silhouettes of the faithful, bundled mummies did not move. So this is what my March madness had come to, I thought. Thirty-two. Father of four. Lover of Flick and Marinaro and Gordon. Fly-tier. Caster of the delicate dry fly. And yet here I was, every muscle throbbing, frozen, sniffing the oil and grime of the car in the middle of a blastedly cold night. It had come to this!

At five-thirty I woke Mort. We each had a plate

of four eggs and a double order of bacon at the diner, and then I washed with vigor, combed my hair back flat and wet, brushed my teeth, and emerged a new man.

" 'Morning is when I am awake and there is a dawn in me,' " I recited loudly. All the sleepy faces in the diner began to lift and scrutinize me warily. They were ready for any sudden psychopathic gesture on my part. " 'Moral reform is the effort to throw off sleep.' " Mort nudged me sharply in the ribs. " 'To be awake is to be alive. I have never yet met a man who was quite awake. How could I have looked him' "—Mort paid the check and began to hustle me (condescendingly, I thought) out of the diner—" 'in the face?' "

An hour later, line frozen at the guides, night crawler silvery with frost and stiff as a pretzel, snow water up to my thigh, I was ready—unlike the pugnacious Henry Thoreau—to be one of those millions who were still slumbering, one of those who with sleep would stand a fair chance of surviving the day. I did not think I would. Skunked. Skunked most miserably on the Big Bend of the East Branch on Opening Day. Was it possible? It would have been humiliating, but it was already nine-thirty and, not having slept, I could hardly stand, let alone be humiliated.

Mort induced me to leave and we headed up Route 22 toward the Ten Mile, tired and blinking. Everywhere the water was outrageously high, flooding into the fields; everywhere the banks were crowded with hunched or hopping mummies. Several bundles of clothing said they had taken "a few," but they turned out to be red suckers. The fish.

Dogged, persistent, half-crazed, I pressed Mort to return to the East Branch—old faithful. Perhaps they *had* stocked the section just below the Sodom Reservoir, like the gargoyle on the bridge had told us what now seemed eight weeks earlier.

When we got there, the splendid crowd suggested that they had indeed stocked. Fishermen lined both sides of the shallow sluice down from the reservoir, one every yard or less, cheek to jowl, some fishing with spinning rods, others with block-busting salt-water gear, some with plain old bait-casting equipment, a few with fly-rods. One madman in earmuffs was giving it a go with dry flies on the flood.

It was the classic Opening Day scene. It was sobering. Yet no one, it seemed, had caught a thing or had a nibble.

But then we found the hero of the day, amid a large admiring crowd: a seventeen-year-old replete with fireman's boots, tri-cornered hat, and gas lamp. His wicker creel, happily opened for all to see, displayed a limit of brookies. All ten barely covered the bottom area. Some were no larger than five inches. He claimed he had taken forty from midnight until seven at his "secret pool" and then, we had to assume, had spent the rest of the morning displaying his trophies.

"It's skill and persistence," he advised us philosophically. "I threw back the small ones."

I was beaten.

Two hours later I felt the car stopping, opened both eyes rapidly, widely, and shouted—irrationally and unaccountably shrilly—"Thank God! We've made it!"

Mort helped collect up all my tackle and clothes. They were in a tangled mass. I put his furniture blanket over my head and began to walk away. He hauled it back and the two of us nearly collapsed on the pavement.

"This is hell," said Mort.

"No, only penance," I said.

As I reached back spasmodically to grasp a night crawler working its moist way down my spine, I saw my wife and children standing on the stoop. For some reason they were unable to say a word. Even my four remarkably vocal children were stark silent. I stuck my tongue out at them, and two scurried behind my wife.

Then, giving Mort two heavy-hearted cheers, I smiled weakly and tried to find strength enough to walk up the six small stairs. I barely made it.

As an afterthought, I turned and called: *"One carp! foul-hooked!"* But the car was already lurching forward, Mort hunched stiffly behind the wheel.

Mari took my elbow as I mounted the last step, shook her head in a downright kindly fashion, braced me, and asked: "Well, where are the trout?"

I was too happy to answer. I was unhooked. I had taken the cure.

3/The Rich Diversity of Spring

Nothing is so beautiful as spring—
When weeds, in wheels, shoot long and
lovely and lush . . .

The glassy peartree leaves and blooms,
they brush
The descending blue; that blue is all
in a rush
With richness . . .
—GERARD MANLEY HOPKINS

"All in a rush/With richness." Yes. That is the spring. Full of diversity. Full of quick change. Full.

One day the streams are high and roiled and brown, and a week later they have become hospitable. One week the trees are still black with winter, the next they are spotted with white-green buds. The forsythia clusters its gold along the slope of the hillocks; skunk cabbage shoots up, "long and lovely and lush."

Worms, spinners, streamers, wet flies, and dries all have their appropriate moment. Spring is not predictable. The Quill Gordon, harbinger of the fly-man's day, may not arrive until late April, the Hendrickson not until late June. I have seen early April crowded with a lush rise of cream Cahills.

One hot April night, when Clyde and Mort and I (in our mid teens then) had camped beside the Big Bend, we saw a momentous three-o'clock hatch in the moonlight of such cream Cahills. They rose and were trapped in the branches of our favorite fallen tree and the trout were leaping a full foot to pluck them out, hanging in mid-air like a fine basketball player with sky-hooks. I saw them.

And later that same night we saw trout crashing through the shallows after a horde of dace. The moon was bright and that was the first time I saw a bona fide case of trout madness.

The three of us had begun to fish about midnight. We were fishing worms, first near the bottom and then, when the trout began to leap to the branches, without even one split shot. The late night was magnificently alive: crickets whistled incessantly, the moon was exceptionally bright, our little fire crackled crisply, we shared and ate sandwiches and chattered away, and then, about three o'clock, the trout, all over a foot long, began to leap into the air for the Cahills. Mort and I continued to fish worms for them—what else, besides spinners, did we then know?—trying to work the bait close into the tangle of branches. The trout would not touch our bait.

Clyde, who was already more sophisticated than we, began to fish flies with a plastic spinning bubble—cursing loudly that he had not brought his fly rod. He cast deftly in toward the branches and around the branches for a full fifteen minutes.

But he got not a touch.

Then, abruptly, the trout stopped rising and we retreated to the fire for hot coffee and a round of excited talk about what we had seen. Obviously we had learned a lesson about the fallibility of the worm. It was sobering. We probably would have learned it sooner, but we sort of believed in those days that the trout season ended in early May, and confined our efforts after that to salt water and bass and pickerel.

Mort was not convinced. Though I had not yet seen a single trout caught on a fly, I had read about it frequently enough, for I read everything I could find on trouting. Flies indeed seemed likely. Clyde

THE SEASONABLE ANGLER

ranted on about the innumerable trout he had
taken on the Beaverkill on flies, and insisted that in
its season it was the deadliest of lures. "Deadliest"
was one of his favorite words.

Just when he was completing a fascinating lie
about a three-pound rainbow that had eluded him
on the Esopus, the water downstream in the shallows began to boil. We scurried along the bank and
there in the moonlight we could distinctly see several fine fifteen- or sixteen-inch trout crashing
through schools of dace.

In the bright moonlit stream we also saw a genuinely massive hook-jawed old brown prowling
in no more than five inches of water. He was
a horse: the biggest trout we'd ever seen. Every
now and then he would slither between several
rocks, jam himself a bit, and turn, slashing onto his
side. He seemed in no hurry to leave the tight
area, but was obviously having a great deal of trou-
ble maneuvering.

"He's mine," said Clyde in a strange, hoarse
voice. "I'm going to hang him."

The words had a common touch of ferocity and
we knew we could not stop him.

He patiently tried spinners, streamers, buck-
tails, worms, live dace, hair flies, a Flatfish, and

even a huge Crazy Crawler—without a strike. He almost snagged the fish with the Flatfish.

And then he picked up five smooth stones from the stream bed, tucked them into his creel, and, as David, went after that giant, winging his missiles with a vindictiveness, a desperation, that frightened Mort and me. He scooped at it madly with his net. He kicked the water. He plunged headlong into that narrow, shallow area, landing right on his chest, and grappled for it with his bare hands. Had he dynamite, I scarcely doubt that he would have used it.

But the brown escaped.

Large and clumsy and distracted as the great fish was, the moonstruck Clyde was clumsier. Or perhaps the trout was simply lucky.

Others—scores of others—were less fortunate. For Clyde was a lethal angler. I once saw him take a fine three-pound rainbow in late spring from a feeder creek leading into the Esopus; the fish must have been stranded after its spawning run, for I have known that creek to drop suddenly. The water was glassy, and he hung it with a 6X leader and a live stone fly nymph (it was illegal to use them then, too). He'd fished over it for an hour with flies, then delicately dapped for it with the live bait on a #22 gold-plated hook. It took him forty-five minutes of dazzling inching and nudging to bring it to net. Or rather, to "chest": for he fell full body on it in the shallows and it did not escape. I saw him kill limits of trout literally dozens of times.

The whole phenomenon of Clyde is compounded in my mind with the phenomenon of spring, for through my adolescence I invariably fished with him in April and May, and stood in awe, amusement, wonder, and despair at his tactics. Together we explored a hundred streams within a hundred miles of New York, hitchhiking to them, training, busing, and then tramping their lengths.

I still prize those little unnamed Catskill creeks he could turn up, those fruitful backwoods stretches on heavily fished streams. I often fish them now myself, with flies, and many of them are still surprisingly good—still filled with those bright eight- to ten-inch browns and brookies, some native. Clyde had an uncanny and unerring nose for trout, and a tremendous energy for exploration, a "romantic readiness" for the unknown and unfished pockets and riffles beyond the hill and into the woods that held rare and sweet prizes. He was the Gatsby of the streams.

Or the Flask—somehow thinking that the trout had personally and hereditarily affronted him; and that it was a sort of point of honor with him to destroy them whenever encountered.

Clyde. Clyde. It was not, somehow, a fisherman's name. Not, surely not, a trout-fisher's name. Yet trout-fisher he was, and a deadly one.

He did not have what you would call style, for he would kill a trout any way and any time. And he was competitive as hell, forever sniffing around our creels and checking other people's stringers. The first monster any of us saw was a six-pound brown that had come out of Kensico Reservoir. Clyde saw it first, half alive and dangling at the end of a stringer along with several perch, a bullhead, and four or five crappies; its owner was several yards away. Clyde ran to it, hoisted the whole stringer out, held it at arm's length, and cried: "By damn! By damn! And with trash fish!" When the man saw him, he dropped his rod and came rushing over, screaming obscenities.

Clyde slammed that huge trout back down into the water and raced off in his waders. The man fortunately paused to examine his catch and Clyde escaped.

Clyde could fish around the clock, from midnight until late the next afternoon, without a touch of fatigue. And then, the trouting over, he would collapse on the train, hang his wet socks over the handle of his chair and into the aisle, hang his bare feet into the aisle also, and snore merrily.

His closet was an arsenal, and he was forever, with every nickel he earned, buying new rods, trying new spinning and fly lines, experimenting with the tying of new flies.

The only thing Clyde liked almost as much as fishing was girls.

Even when we were in our early teens, before any of us had a car, he would talk all the long morning up on the milk train to Brewster about conquests and possibilities, shapes and expectations. That is, when he was not talking about trout.

Mort and I were still much more devoted to simpler crafts and sports, but Clyde fascinated us for he brought the same enthusiasm to girls that he brought to trout. I don't think I ever heard him speak about anything else: not books or baseball or politics or religion, though he once muttered obscenities about golf.

It was inevitable, I suppose, that he soon began taking girls fishing with him—and it was then that Mort and I began to make separate plans. But where in Brooklyn he found such a variety of

striking girls (for he was as homely and success-
ful as Buck Duke) to tramp the Long Island shores
for snappers and fluke, the Catskills for trout, the
reservoirs for white perch, to fish with him on an
icy April morning at the Big Bend at five o'clock,
I cannot speculate. They'd troop along obediently,
sit patiently by, leap up and down in their cash-
mere sweaters when a trout was on, abide our
incessant trout talk, and then, on the trips back,
snuggle up close to old homely Clyde—and neck.

It was disconcerting.

A girl was there the last time I saw Clyde,
though it was not she who caused our final break.

One day while fishing with him on the Amawalk, when it was still open water, a very solid
brookie struck my C. P. Swing as I fished it up into
a fast run and flirted it back, letting it work deep
into the socket of the pool. The fish fought
briskly, and several times I saw it turn and
burrow down into the swirling water. It was a
gorgeous male, well over a foot, and I could see the
bright markings and sleek form distinctly as it
struggled in the Amawalk's lovely auburn water.
The spinning reel is a tough instrument to beat,
and in a few moments I netted it.

Instinctively I thought of breaking its neck and
placing it with several smaller browns already in

my creel. But the stream was small and low and it was already mid-May and I thought that perhaps I would fish it again that month and it would be good to know that there was a big fish astream.

I had seen such streams decline sharply in the years we fished them—pummeled during those first few weeks of the season. But I had never seen a trout released.

I unfastened the treble hooks carefully. Slowly, hesitantly, I began to turn out my net.

"What are you doing?" cried Clyde, pounding up in his heavy waders, an Arlene by his side.

"I think I'll return this one," I said quietly.

"Return it? He's *returning* the trout, Arlene! He's throwing back a fifteen-inch brook trout!"

The girl nodded and smiled. She did not recognize the significance of the event. Clyde rushed to my side and, as I began to lower the net again, took my hand forcefully.

"Do you know what you're doing, man?" He was dumbstruck.

I merely looked at him, more intent now on doing what had been a simple act of increasing my future pleasure.

"You've lost your mind. Hasn't he, Arlene?"

"I guess he can return it if he wants to," Arlene said simply.

[74]

Clyde let go of my hand and took a step back.

The large fish lay dormant now in the net, its bright red gills opening wide and slowly, the "rose moles all in stipple" upon its mottled back. Without touching it with my hand, I pushed the net further into the water and then gently urged the trout up and free from the cords. A gill caught and I carefully worked it loose.

"Wait," said Clyde. "If you don't want it, I'll . . ."

But it was too late. I had already slipped the fish free and back into its element. It now began to waver slowly and then the current caught it and it turned downstream, and then it waveringly headed up and into the depth of the little pool.

This was all too much for Clyde. He promptly packed up, put his arm around Arlene, and walked off. We haven't spoken since.

For me, it seemed like the beginning of something.

And it was.

For not many years later, one spring day when a brisk Hendrickson hatch was on the water, I took my first trout on a fly, and I saw it was possible, and then I traded my spinning rod and all my lures and lost my heart to bamboo and a hat full of feathers.

And angling became for me more than a pursuit of conquest, more even than a sport.

Often my skeptical wife asks me about the fascination, the involvement, the seriousness of my marriage to angling. And I tell her about a trout stream in May, when the Hendricksons begin to come off the water gingerly—one or two a minute, and then in clusters. I tell her something about the permutations and combinations of it all, the varieties of water, the knowledge of where trout will lie, the subtle differences in a dozen brands of a trout's rise, the factors of time and weather, the feel of fine bamboo, the sight of a long line arcing back and dropping a foot beyond the circle of a rise, the water suddenly boiling or dimpling as the trout takes, the sudden firm feel of that thing out there, connecting you to one of the elements. I tell her about the lush skunk cabbage in mid-April, the soft banks, the stages of budding, the feel of inching upstream against the current in the Willowemoc or the Schoharie or the Esopus, and hawking the surface for feeding fish. I tell her about the soft-fluttering cream Cahills coming off the Amawalk an hour before dusk and the promise of big browns; I mention memories and changes and hopes and the chill dusk of a May evening on the upper Beaverkill. I tell her what Emerson says: "Every object rightly seen unlocks a new faculty of the soul." There are many "objects" astream.

Several times she has fallen asleep during my diatribes and I know perhaps the largest truth of this business of angling: it is private, and teaches privateness and the quiet satisfaction of something sweet and full inside.

What the angler knows he knows in hand and eye and bone. The endless repetitions of a cast—what do they build in arm and eye? The innumerable floats of a fly? The particular studied flirt of a streamer in slow or fast, deep or shallow, pocketed or flat water on a drizzly May morning—can this be reduced to maxims, appreciations? "Only so much I know," says Emerson, "as I have lived." Only so much I know of angling as I have angled and dreamt angling.

It is pragmatic. And metaphysical.

Most often in those early springs of fly-fishing, since no one taught me, I learned by necessity. I learned the roll cast one long afternoon on the bushy Amawalk when there were trout rising and no room for a back cast. I learned how to drift a nymph—and appreciate the nymph—one almost frustrating evening near the Beaverkill campsite when the bulges were tails, not lips. I learned to

[77]

release trout when I saw that taking them indiscriminately would deplete fishing for all time thenceforth. I learned to approximate a hatch when I saw that there is a time for the Hendrickson, the Quill Gordon, the Cahill, the March Brown—that it is not a random but a lawful business.

The eye and mind—and the fish—are ennobled by fly-fishing.

One late-May afternoon not long after I had first begun to fly-fish, I was on a small stream fishing dries upstream. The day was warm and slightly overcast; the water, coming from the bottom of a reservoir several miles upstream, was pleasantly in the high fifties. I had expected a good hatch, but no flies were coming off the water and I had fished for four hours on the top without a strike. What made it most frustrating was that fish were everywhere present. You could see them streaking across the pools wildly, splashing the surface thunderously. But what were they taking?

Finally I switched to wet flies and then to nymphs. Patiently, carefully, I fished downstream —retrieving in short erratic jerks—and upstream with nymphs, dead drift. I tried dark patterns against the clarity of the stream, the March Brown and the Adams, in sizes #10 to #18; I tried Light

Cahills in similar sizes; and I tried attractor patterns, large and small—the wet Hair Coachman that has always produced well for me, and the Parmachene Belle. Nothing.

Nor did matters change as the evening grew on and the slight wind died. A few creamy Cahills came off the water, a few small Iron Blue Duns. But I saw no trout rise to them, and none rose to my imitations, even in the smallest sizes. Yet the splashing and the frantic darting across pools continued, and it was not until just before dusk that a #12 White Wulff, bouncing pertly through a riffle, finally took a nice twelve-inch brown.

I wet my hands, gently removed the hook, and was about to return the fish when several small objects plopped out of its mouth. They were greenish-yellow, about an inch in length, a bit squashed, but quite recognizable. Of course. Leaf-rollers.

I had heard about such days but never experienced one, when trout will touch nothing that imitates a water-born insect. Even the one brown I had taken on a White Wulff might well have mistaken the large bushy fly for a moth.

My schedule was tight that spring and I did not get out on this water again until late June. By that time there were no signs of the erratic behavior I had witnessed, and I took four nice browns on a large spent-wing Adams between six-thirty and dusk on the same stream. The stream had returned to normal. The perplexing frenzy had vanished.

But sometimes through that winter, I brooded about the leafrollers and several times stopped into the more knowledgeable fly-tackle dealers to talk about them. I was shown a few imitations, but was satisfied with only one: the Schwiebert Leafroller. The others, usually only yellow-green wool tied around the shank of a #12 or #14 short- or long-shank hook, appealed to me so little that I was convinced they'd appeal to the trout even less (a supposition that several springs later proved quite true). I bought four Schwieberts, two each of a number of less interesting patterns, and a variety of materials with which to try my own: chartreuse wool, yellow wool, dark-green wool, yellow chenille, several shades of green chenille, and—to experiment—some red, blue, and black chenille. If they'd touch my creations at all, this might be a good time to see how well trout could distinguish color.

It is a special delight to catch trout on flies you have tied yourself, and though the standard patterns deftly tied will always produce best, it is part of the curiosity of anglers to experiment.

I tied some forty or fifty leafrollers that winter, in about a dozen different varieties. Several I tied simply by wrapping wool around the shank, without a tail; others had a short tail of dyed impala tail, to impart some motion; several had quarter-inch tails of green wool; and for several others I left a quarter inch of wool loose beyond the head as well as the tail. (On the last, I tied off with black or dark-brown thread to simulate the head.) I also tied a series of chenille leafrollers, using the same variations, though this time I tied the chenille directly to the shank rather than wrapping it around. These I tied in all colors. In addition, in an attempt to make a floating leafroller, I tied a dozen worms with several twists of small light-ginger hackle around their bodies.

I had a number of opportunities to fish several streams in early and middle June that spring but —whether because of rains or frost—there were no leafrollers to be seen. I tried the commercial patterns and my own on several afternoons, when the defined hatches were over, but with no leafrollers near the water I had absolutely not a tap.

And the next spring family and school commitments kept me off the stream during the most likely weeks. I listened carefully to several reports, usually by disgruntled dry-fly men, about the leafrollers on various streams, during my periodic lunch-hour visits to the tackle shops, but never had a chance to try my own creations.

I prefer to take my trout on the dry fly whenever I can, using all the trout-sense I can muster to see how and on what the trout are feeding, then imitating the natural as closely as I can in size and color and pattern, and finally presenting the fly in the most pleasant manner—upstream. I like the "lawfulness" of the classic hatches, the technical problems of "matching the hatch," accurate presentation to feeding fish, the avoidance of drag; but most, I think, I enjoy the incomparable rise, the abrupt opening of the stream, the dramatic splash, the electricity from stream to eye to hand. All this did not seem the course my leafroller fishing would take. Still, I was curious.

The next year I hit the stream at the height of the leafroller activity and, seeing the little critters all over, was astounded that I had missed them my first time on those waters. We are indeed bound by habit; I had looked for flies coming off the water because that's what I wanted to see. I had not seen the leafrollers—though they must have been there in great numbers—simply because there was no thought to look for them.

Well, there was no doubt about their existence

that day, and for over an hour I simply watched them and the trout taking them in several pools. There is no substitute for such scrutiny, and it should become a regular habit for trout-fishers to long observe the water before wetting a line (though, as Thoreau knew, too many of us Americans have a kind of St. Vitus' Dance, on as well as off the stream—an itch for action).

The little green worms were on the leaves and hanging by gossamer threads from the leaves. Frequently they would drop slowly on their threads and hang suspended only a few inches above the water. Several times I saw fat fourteen- or fifteen-inch browns leap half their length out of the water (and hang there) to cop these worms. But most times the worm would fall in and glide—wriggling and squirming—a yard or more downstream until it was taken. A number of times I could see trout streak or flash in the clear late-May water, and I suspect they were gulping drowned or sunken leafrollers. These sunken worms are hard to see, particularly if there is any sun on the water and even with Polaroid glasses, but much more activity actually takes place here during the leafroller weeks—though it is the surface activity that is most dramatic.

The trout would take the surface leafrollers

greedily and without hesitation, with a kind of slurping, dramatic rise. There was little haste except when the water beneath a low-hanging branch would literally boil with motion as two or three trout in shallow water would thrash about after them. Nor did these trout spook like those during a standard rise. Before casting my first fly that day, I waded to midstream noisily and grasped a few worms from their threads. The trout kept rising within a few yards of me and, when I tossed a worm several feet upstream and a little to the right, a fine trout took it no more than a foot from my waders. I splashed the water with my hand, tried again, and the same thing happened.

That day was extraordinary. I took fifteen or sixteen trout, all on leafrollers of various patterns, and returned them all carefully to the water. I took them in a host of different ways, too: downstream, upstream on the surface, and upstream dead drift, several inches beneath the surface. One of the most interesting ways to take them is directly downstream, if your position is correct in the stream, when the worm has risen with the force of the current to the surface and dangles there, wriggling in the water; this seems to represent to the trout a real leafroller hanging suspended on its gossamer thread. The leader, of course, can even rise up out of the water in this method, and I suspect that the best way to fish this way would be with one of those old twelve-foot greenheart rods on a short line, possibly one that was all leader; the French method of dapping that I observed used with killing effect in the Alps would also serve well here. I recommend neither.

The usual way to fish the leafroller, I've since learned, is like a wet fly, across and downstream. But this method appealed to me least because it required the least concentration, the least care in initial presentation. You could simply meander leisurely downstream, roll-casting your line out after it had been floated and then jiggled a few times. Much more water can be covered this way. Actually, though, I had fewer strikes fishing the leafroller like a wet fly, perhaps because the drag, though less noticeable beneath the water, still destroyed the natural drift of a creature with no real power of locomotion in water. Several times when my line merely dangled and my eyes were scanning the water for surface activity upstream, I felt a sharp tug and found that a trout had hooked itself.

The most demanding way to fish the leafroller is unquestionably upstream, dead drift or with very slight taps. As for nymph fishing, the rod should be held high, slack line kept to a minimum, and a keen eye leveled at the line for the slightest twitch or abnormal movement. Rarely is the strike itself seen, rarely felt: it is all an eye-on-line game.

But it gave me the greatest pleasure to take a few fish on the surface that day, as it has on subsequent days during the few weeks annually of frantic leafroller activity.

There were, to begin with, problems getting the artificial worm to float. None of the commercial flies I tried would stay afloat, and even when doused with a dry-fly preparation my wool inchworms would not, of course, stay on the surface more than a few seconds. Only the chenille flies I'd tied with a few turns of hackle around the body and loose chenille at each end would stay up; silicone improved their float considerably. But these produced far fewer fish than any other fly. Two trout, both small, rose and took it that day— one with green chenille, the other with red!—but there was clearly far less action. Still, it was pleasant work to take something on the top on my own creations—and good to know they could be taken this way.

I saw a good number of trout rise short to my floating chenille leafroller, and suspect they scrutinize a surface imitation more closely than they do a wet pattern. An improved version of this floater has taken some fine trout for me since then, and I am convinced that a decent floating leaf-roller can still be made.

I have since tied several dozen other varieties of leafrollers, and find myself, at least in this case, more interested in the number of kinds of flies that will take trout than in perfecting a single pattern or two. Leafroller fishing for me is somehow an engaging game, and quite distinct from the special delights of fishing a hatch.

Since I have caught far fewer trout on leaf-rollers without a loose tail, I rarely use the commercial brands, which are tied only to the shank. I always leave that quarter-inch of loose wool or chenille at the end to float free and wriggle with the current. And I always seal the end of this loose material with several drops or dabs of clear head lacquer, for otherwise it shreds and looks highly improbable in the water. Most of my flies now also have this loose material extending beyond the head. A yellow-green (almost a yellow) seems to be the most consistent producer, though all colors—including red, black, blue, and orange— have taken fish for me. Which does not precisely resolve the color question, does it?

I've met avid dry-fly men who moan when they hear that the leafrollers have taken over their favorite stretch. But that wild week or two has added a new dimension to my spring, and I look forward with a special excitement to those days when the trout will touch nothing else.

They are part of the great variety of spring— the rich rush of varying modalities that work their way through the season with the most marvelous and mysterious lawfulness.

4/Family Interludes

He that views the ancient ecclesiastical
canons shall find hunting to be forbidden
to churchmen, as being a toilsome,
perplexing recreation; and shall find angling
allowed to clergymen, as being a harmless
recreation, a recreation that invites them
to contemplation and quietness.

—IZAAK WALTON

Though the relationship of
an avid fisherman to his family
may be said to have no season, or to be always "in season," it reaches the peak of its
intensity—or aggravation—in the very height of
the trouter's year.

There are, I am sure, innumerable arcane and
esoteric reasons for this.

But the safe pragmatic reason is simply this: the
trout-fisher is at his moment of greatest self- and
trout-absorption—and least resistance; and his family, flourishing under the beneficence of his year-

long support and devotion, and the ideal weather, is at maximum strength.

Days are long; children are indefatigable; wives acquire an alarming propensity for shopping and house-hunting and "just walking together, like a *real* family, in the park." In the early days I did not have an ally among them, and my secret fishing life suffered much at the hands of my family.

There were the little things: two missing barred-rock necks that turned up under Anthony-the-thief's pillow; a notorious departure from the Schoharie in the midst of a massive Hendrickson hatch, after I had waited three hours for it to appear (my wife called them "Morgans" and pleaded that we leave "this bug-infested place"); innumerable engagements that took precedence; irony; caustic wit to the effect that "grown men" did not act in the ridiculous way I acted about trout. I must be painfully truthful about it, for it all reached a crisis, a momentous crisis, in an incident still painful to recall.

My fishing friends say I am too generous with women and little children. Perhaps. For I suppose Mari, Paul, Charles, Jennifer, and Anthony owe their survival of that Fathers' Day trip to my extraordinary equanimity. I am not at all sure how I survived.

The spring, troutless and city-bound that year, had been long, but Fathers' Day weekend was longer.

We left in a flurry, all six of us, on Friday, but despite my best efforts, my speed and my scheming, it was still too late even to make the latest moments of the evening rise on the closest streams. So I settled into a family habit of mind, decided to bide my good time, and set about enjoying a harmless day of visiting friends and swimming on Saturday. After that we could easily fulfill the most prominent of our trip's simple purposes: as I had engineered my wife into saying, "A few solid hours of fly-fishing for Dad—poor Dad, who never gets out on the streams anymore because he loves us so much."

Not that I believed her, or had much confidence that at this particular season of my married life I would actually get to drop a few flies—but her gesture seemed sincere and I took it at face value. "A turning point," I thought with quiet satisfaction. Thus, hopefully, I had stashed my little Thomas and my vest carefully in the corner of our rented station wagon. I had heard of such turning points.

The temperature was ninety-eight degrees when we left our friends at three o'clock that Saturday: too hot to fish, no doubt, so I allowed Mari to persuade me that Vermont would be cooler, that we would have time to fish that evening and all day Sunday. "A nice drive will keep us cool," she insisted.

It was little less than one hundred and fifty degrees in the car once we hit the crowded highway: I cannot remember being able to drive faster than thirty-five. But up Routes 5 and then 91 to Brattleboro we went, pausing to examine, while we sped, a half dozen or more promising waterways. It had been part of my plan (cunningly conceived, I must admit) to inject my oldest son, Paul, with the trout fever, and the serum had taken with a vengeance. Before I could see a stream, he'd spot one and call out, "Can we stop here, Dad? It looks like a terrific place for tremendous trout."

He did this several dozen times.

The serum nearly cracked me.

By the time we reached Vermont, all four children were howling wildly, stepping on each other's toes and pride and souls. Dinner took two hours, motel-hunting another hour, and precisely at dusk we were established in cool Vermont, exhausted. Had I been on the Schoharie, at Hendrickson time, I would not have been able to lift my arm to cast.

"Tomorrow we'll get some big ones," I said to

Paul as we turned off the lights and settled, all six of us, into the quiet and cool of the air-conditioned room.

"Do you promise, Dad?"

"I promise," I said.

"Can I get some big ones, too?" asked Anthony, my four-year-old, in the dark room.

"Maybe."

"Me too?" asked Charles with his fog-horn voice. "If Paul does, I want to get some big ones, too."

"Let's sleep now, children."

It was quiet for five full minutes and, motionless, pooped, I was nearly into a pleasant dream about the Green drake hatch on the Beaverkill when Jennifer whispered loudly, "You'll let me catch some big ones too, won't you, Daddy?"

"Shussssh!" said my wife. And then, sardonically, "*Trout!*"

Well, Sunday it was raining long thick droplets of rain: a day-long pernicious rain if I'd ever seen one.

"Didn't you say fishing was best in the rain, Dad?" asked Paul.

"You *wouldn't* take the boy out in a rain like this, would you, Nick?" asked Mari.

"Not when it's heavy, Paul," I said quietly.

"And you *wouldn't* expect the rest of us to sit in a muggy car while you were out catching pneumonia, would you?"

"We will not fish in this weather," I assured my wife, sullenly.

"You promised, Dad!"

"It will not rain all day," I told Paul. "And maybe it's not raining in New York State."

So we drove and we sang a hundred songs and we munched some of our genuine Vermont maple sugar—which did not quite justify Saturday's trip to cool Vermont, and which made Jennifer dreadfully nauseous—and we made our way slowly through the blinding Fathers' Day rain that was sure to kill any decent fly-fishing for a full three days, along the winding, twisting Molly Stark Trail, and the children stopped singing, and then fought and bellowed, and Mari became irritated and blamed me, and then Paul blamed me for not finding him a "dry trout stream."

We crossed into New York, where it was pouring nails, at about twelve-thirty, had a long lunch, and then started gloomily, for a Fathers' Day—or any day—down Route 22. The Hoosic River, I noted, was impossibly brown, and the rain still showed no signs of growing less frantic. The Green River, a sprightly spring-fed creek, was clearer, but the rain continued and Mari would have none of sitting in a muggy car while I got pneumonia.

"If you could find us a nice clean beach, where we could get some sun and have something to do for an hour or so . . . But you really can't expect me . . ."

"Scarcely," I said.

"You promised," said Paul.

A disaster either way. Straight home: the only solution.

There is absolutely no question in my mind that I should indeed have gone home. Right then. Tragedy was imminent. Had I simply read the signs of the times, I could have avoided disaster.

Yes, blithely I was heading home, peace in my soul, capitulation painless, when, as we approached Brewster, the sun broke out suddenly—brightly, fetchingly. I could not resist a quick look at the Sodom section of the East Branch of the Croton River.

"We won't do any fishing," I promised. "I just want a fast look at an old friend. I used to fish this stream when I was a kid, every Opening Day. Came up the first time when I was . . ."

"Thirteen. I know. You mention it every time we pass this silly creek."

"Do I really? Do I mention it *every* time we pass?"

"Yes, you do. 'I used to fish the Left Branch of the Croydon every Opening Day when I was a kid.' Every time."

"East Branch. Croton," I muttered. "A short look. Three minutes. Perhaps less."

"I sincerely hope less."

Miraculously, the water below and above the bridge was admirably clear, not crystal but a translucent auburn, perhaps because it traveled to this point over a long cobblestone sluice after shooting down from the top of the reservoir. Interesting, I thought; very interesting.

I scurried back to the car with the happy news.

"Well, if you think you can catch a few trout for supper," Mari said, "you can drop Anthony and me off at a coffee shop for half an hour and take the rest of your children fishing in the Left Branch of the Croydon, or whatever it is."

"*All* of them?"

"I want to go with Daddy," shouted Jennifer.

"If Paul goes, I have to go too, Dad," said Charles petulantly.

"At least make it forty-five minutes," I said.

"With Anthony? In a coffee shop?"

"All right, children: a half hour to catch two fat trout for supper."

"Nick, you haven't brought home a trout in two years. You talk about fishing day and night; read about it constantly; tie those confounded bugs by the evening; go on and on and on—and never bring home any fish."

Since the clock was running, I did not choose to explain that despite the tragedy of being married I still *caught* trout now and then, though I rarely kept them any more. One such argument, with my mother-in-law, who to this day thinks I keep a mistress on the banks of the "Croydon," led me to stomp out of the room with the profound truism: "Do golfers eat golf balls?"

"Two fat trout for dinner, children—in one half hour."

I dropped my wife off at ten of five, spent seven minutes acquiring some night crawlers, another four setting up Paul's spinning rod, and was on the stream by one minute after five exactly.

"Lovely," I said. "The water's beautiful, Paul. We're going to get four or five."

"Really, Dad?"

"Can't miss. Look: that fellow right under the bridge has one—see him splashing?"

The children crowded together along the bank, watching the brisk battle of a thrashing and leaping eleven-inch brown. I took the time to sneak in six or seven casts, but did not even get a tap.

Then Paul wanted the rod and I gave it to him, telling him how to cast across and slightly upstream, how to hold the rod tip down in anticipation of the strike, how to keep delicate control of the moving bait. He managed his casts well, and I watched eagerly as the night crawler floated downstream and out of sight. Before his fourth cast, Charles wanted his turn too. No, I had promised Paul he'd catch a trout first, I told him gently.

"I want *my* turn, Daddy," said Jennifer.

"We only have one rod."

"No fair. It's not fair, Dad," said Charles gruffly.

"Can't you keep these infants quiet so I can fish?" demanded Paul.

"Don't get nasty," I advised.

"They're bothering me, Dad."

"After Paul gets a fish," I promised Jennifer and Charles wisely, "you two get a turn each."

"Only one," said Jennifer.

"Two trout," said Paul.

But he got no strikes in the next fourteen or fifteen casts, and I noticed that it was now five-eighteen. I was glad I'd left my Thomas in the car. Another ten minutes of this madness—no more.

To get the younger children out of Paul's way, I decided to go up on the bridge itself for the last few minutes, though I noted with alarm how fast the cars sped by. I flattened the children against the edge, warned them sharply not to climb up the low wall, and leaned far over to peer down into the fairly clear auburn water.

A few flies were coming off the water—small darkish flies—but I paid them no heed.

Then I saw it: a long dark shadow, nose upstream, slightly to the left of a large submerged boulder. Now and then it would rise slowly to the right or left and, almost imperceptibly, break the surface of the flat stream. The fish was well over a foot long.

I tried to point it out to Jennifer and Charles, lifting one in each arm so both could see at exactly the same time, but when they scrambled further onto the low wall I spooked and put them back on the pavement, whereupon they raced back and forth across the bridge several times while cars shot by menacingly.

I told Paul about the fish and he promptly climbed up the bank and onto the bridge. He plunked his worm loudly down into the water and it bobbed to the surface and waved there, without the slightest threat of ever being disturbed by a trout.

But the long trout kept rising, once or twice every minute—God, was it really five twenty-three already?—and when I tossed it several bits of a worm, it swirled and snapped at them, though it did not finally take any.

Then a few of the small darkish flies rose to my level and I leaned out incautiously and grabbed several of them.

Dark blue; tiny. Most curious.

What were they? Iron Blue Duns. Not more than three or four a minute, but a steady hatch. *Acentrella*—about #18. Weren't they a late-April Mayfly, though? No matter. *Acentrella*—nothing else.

Not much of a dinner, but the long trout was unmistakably settling for them. Had I tied a few last winter? Yes, one each, a #18 and a #16.

The trout rose again—and then again, this time with a definite sucking-down of the water, a turning of its sleek yellow body that showed it to be of considerable size and weight.

Five twenty-eight.

I could stand it no longer. Grabbing Jennifer

and Charles by the collars, I rushed back to the car, plucked out my aluminum rod case and vest, and then tugged the children—silent, frightened—down the muddy bank, past a flourishing garden of shiny poison ivy, and toward the downstream section below the bridge.

Swiftly I unhoused and jointed my delicate Thomas, a simple, lovely idea in bamboo. I managed to mount the fly reel and slip the line through the first two guides, but then began to fumble. The line slipped back through to the reel. Then I worked the line through four guides and discovered that it was twisted around the rod after the second. Then it was through all of them, but the spidery 6X tippet would not shake loose and got tangled in itself, and I had to select another. Then I couldn't find my Iron Blue Dun in #18. Should I try the # 16? Or an Adams in #18? Or a small Leadwing Coachman?

Finally I found the Blue in with the Adamses, its hackles a bit bent, and I poked the film of head lacquer out after only six or seven tries and then knotted the fly to the leader on my fourth attempt.

Five thirty-five. She should be furious already—even on Fathers' Day.

"Quiet. You children have got to be absolutely quiet. Not a sound"—they had said nothing—"good

[101]

children. You're not going to spoil Daddy's sixteen-incher, are you?"

"How big is a sixteen-incher, Daddy?"

"Big, Jennifer. Very big. Quiet. Quiet. Quiet,
now."

"PAUL! DADDY'S GOING TO CATCH A
SIXTEEN-INCHER!" Jennifer howled in her
high-pitched shrilly voice.

"Can I help you, Dad?" asked Charles.

Paul, on the bridge, had leaned far over to see the
action. Clouds were forming rapidly in the sky.

"*Paul!* Get back!" I called, nearly flopping
over on the muddy bank. "But WATCH OUT
FOR THE CARS! Not too far back!"

Damn, no waders. No matter. The moment was
here.

I stepped in boldly—in my Fathers' Day shoes,
in my neatly creased trousers, in my Fathers'
Day sport jacket—tumbled to one arm on a mossy
rock, climbed over the riffles slowly, bent my
hand to steady myself on another rock (soaking
the new sports jacket up to the elbow and along the
hemline), and meticulously surveyed the long flat
pool.

A few soft small drops of rain began to fall.

"Paul! Paul! Look what Daddy's doing!"

"Dad, can I go wading, too?" shouted Charles.

"Can we, Daddy?"

"Will all my very good children kindly be ab-so-lute-ly quiet for ten minutes. I love you all. I really do. But *please, please* be quiet."

"Daddy, Daddy," called Jennifer. "Charles is in the water. Charles is in the water. Charles is . . ."

"*I am not! I am not!*"

"Charles! Get out and stay out! Now!"

Another foot. Not too close. Whoops! Almost slipped that time. Don't rain. Don't rain, yet! "Paul! Will you *please* get off that railing?"

"My line's tangled, Dad. And I can't see a thing."

"Then come down. But carefully! Watch out for the cars. And the poison ivy."

"Will you fix my line, Dad?"

"In a minute. In just one minute."

Five *thirty-eight!*

"Charles is in the water. Charles is . . ."

"I am not!"

"Charles, if you don't stay out of the water I'll break your little arm!"

I could not see the fish beside the boulder, but thought that amid the steady raindrops and bubbles on the surface I detected the characteristic dimple of a trout's rise. "Now," I murmured audibly. I looped out several yards of line, checked behind me for trees or shrubs or sons or daughter.

The old feeling. That glorious old feeling. After twelve full months, it was all still there.

One more false cast.

"Now."

The line sped out, long and straight; the leader unfolded; the fly turned the last fold and dropped, quietly, five inches below the base of the bridge. Perfect.

I retrieved line slowly, watching for drag, squinting into the steadily increasing rain, along the rim of the dark water, to see that tiny dark-blue fly. In another moment it would be over the spot.

There was a heavy splash below me. Then another and another.

"Charles is throwing stones, Daddy. Charles is . . ."

"CHARLES!"

Whammo!

The tiny Iron Blue Dun disappeared in a solid sucking down of the water. I raised the rod swiftly, felt the line tighten along its length and hold. Not too hard. Not too hard, Nick. I did not want to snap the 6X leader.

I had him. A good brown. A really good brown. I felt his weight against the quick arcing of my little Thomas. Sixteen inches for sure. Not an inch less. The trout turned, swirled at the surface, and bolted upstream.

"Daddy caught one!" shouted Jennifer.

There were momentous splashes downstream.

"CHARLES!"

Out of the corner of my wet eye I could see Paul, in his short pants, hopping through the great garden of poison ivy. "Got a fish, Dad?" he called.

"Got a big one, kids," I said proudly, holding the Thomas high, reeling in the line before the first guide to fight him from the reel. "Your ol' Dad's got a good one this time—*whoaaa!*"

Just then Paul slipped on the muddy slope and slid rawly—through more poison ivy—to the brink of the stream.

The rain was steady and thick now, and I felt it trickle down past my jacket collar and along my spine.

The trout had run far up under the bridge and I was playing him safely from the reel. Several times he leaped high into the air, shaking, splattering silver in all directions, twisting like a snake.

"I'll help you, Dad," shouted Charles, splashing vigorously toward me.

"Didn't I tell you——?"

But before I finished, the huge trout began to

shoot downstream rapidly, directly toward me. I retrieved line frantically. He was no more than four yards from me and I could see the 6X leader trailing from the corner of his partly opened mouth; the jaw was already beginning to hook.

Charles was quite close to me now, behind me, and I half turned to shoo him back to shore. His hair was plastered flat on his head from the rain, and he had a long thin stick in his hands and was holding it out, in the direction of the trout.

"I'll get him, Dad, I'll get him," he said. His tone was sincere and helpful.

"*No!*" I shouted, and turned to wrest it away from him.

The gesture was too sudden. The leather-soled shoes were no match for the mossy rocks. With gusts of heavy rain pelting my face, I felt my left foot slipping, tried to catch myself and my tangled line, felt my right foot slipping too, and, holding my delicate, my beloved Thomas high overhead, went down, disastrously, flat on my rump, up to my chest, and kept going, the Thomas slamming wildly against a rock . . .

I consider it a holy miracle of the first water that I survived that day.

And I consider it a fine miracle of physics that my

Thomas survived. With only minor scratches.

And I consider it sure evidence of my extraordinary equanimity and good cheer that my family survived. Yet there may well have been a touch of clairvoyance in my ensuing patience: for pragmatically, how could I have known then that Paul would become my favorite fishing partner, Charles a skilled and careful net-man, and that on a memorable June evening I would baptize Mari in the holy waters of the Beaverkill?

Yes, Paul had caught the fever. And the very next year, fishing the little Sawkill near Woodstock, in mid-April, he caught his first trout.

We had taken only one outfit, his spinning rod, and I proceeded to give him some instruction, casting six or seven times up under the bridge. They had not yet stocked the stream but I knew there were always a number of solid holdover browns that survived in the deep ledge-pools.

Since the water was fairly low, I decided it would be best if we went upstream and Paul cast down, so that there would be less chance of the lure snagging on the bottom. He went up on the rocks by himself and cast twice, across and downstream, with no results. The casts were well executed and he retrieved the little C. P. Swing with neat, short jerks.

On the third cast the rod suddenly arced sharply. I thought it was a rock but Paul insisted it was moving.

I didn't believe him until the trout leaped. It was a splendid brown, well over a foot, and all of us—Paul, Charles, Jennifer, and Anthony—began to shout at once.

The fish raced across that little pool wildly. But he was well hooked, the drag gave line when needed, and soon Paul had him up close.

Charles, who was now a properly equipped net-man, slipped the net under the large fish with genuine talent. And we had him.

I grasped the trout around the head and flexed back its neck abruptly. Jennifer flinched and Paul asked me why I had to be so cruel. I told him that this was the quickest way, caused the least pain, and that it kept the trout from secreting bile. "If you're going to keep them," I began, but then realized that it does not occur to a young boy to release what he has caught. Especially not a first trout! That could come later.

It was a splendid event. Charles carried the fish, hung by the jaw from a forked stick, up the hill. Even Mari was impressed.

We took the trout directly to Frank Mele's house, and he treated that first prize with all the ceremony it deserved. First he got out his ruler and measured it out at fourteen and a half inches. Then, with his razor-sharp pocket knife, he showed Paul and Charles how to dress it carefully, showed them how to slit from the vent forward, remove the innards, thumb out the blood clot, and cut out the gills. They were fascinated.

"Now," said Frank, "we'll have to trace it. Just like they do in the fancy sporting clubs."

He got out a strip of butcher paper and Paul laid his fish upon it and traced its outlines with my pen. Below it, Frank advised, Paul should put the vital information.

Years later, the memento of that first trout still hangs proudly in Paul's room. The brown butcher paper is rolling up on the ends but a few silver scales are still stuck to the body area, and beneath the silhouette reads:

brown Troute, 14½ inches
caught by Paul B. Lyons

Sawkille, Woodstock
4/16/67

It seemed at the time the beginning of something.

5 / Mecca

Mecca (mĕk′à), *n.* 1. . . . a holy city;
hence, any place sought, especially by
great numbers of persons, as a supremely
desirable goal.

One spring there was no
spring. March lingered into
mid-April; late April was a wintry February; and by the end of May you might have
been convinced that, since not even the Quill Gordon had arrived, God was taking a special vengeance on fly-fishers. On all except me.

Emergence dates would be postponed; few trout
would be taken in the fly-only stretches I had begun to haunt; June (unless God became ungodly
vengeful toward fly-fishers) would be perfect.
While small clusters of distressed anglers grumbled
in the tackle shops, I gloated. June was the only
time I would be free, and June would be ideal. Even
Brannigan was morose. I was serenely gleeful.

All winter I had corresponded from the city with Mike, a fanatic like myself but one who had taken the plunge and now lived chiefly—and blissfully—for fishing. What other way is there? Brannigan constantly wrote me of his friend Hawkes, a knowledgeable old Catskill trouting genius whom I had never met. But Hawkes was more than knowledgeable, more than a rumor: he was a myth. In an increasing number of understated and sometimes unconcious ways, the old trout fisher—in off seasons, a cellist—began to emerge from Mike's letters as a figure of outrageous proportions. He had, so far as I could tell, a special formula for dyeing leaders to within a chromophore of the color of eight different streams at a dozen different times of the year. He no longer kept emergence tables, but could tell (by extrasensory perception?) not only which fly would be hatching on a particular day, but at what time of the day, even to the hour, the fly would emerge. And in what numbers! Of course I believed none of it. Who would? It was all the fiction of that wild Irishman. Brannigan was obviously a madman, more afflicted even than I, who had lost two jobs because of his trout neurosis, and almost a wife: he was given to exaggeration, fantasy, mirage, and fly-tying. I had only almost lost my wife.

But I was curious. Who wouldn't be? And I had asked four or five times, covertly, whether or not Hawkes would fish with us when I got away for a week in June.

"Rarely fishes any more," wrote Brannigan. "Most streams have become rather easy for him; most hatches too pedestrian. Says he only fishes the Green Drake hatches—says there's still something to be learned there."

The Green Drake, yes—the most exciting and mysterious of them all. *Ephemera guttulata Pictet,* yes, which brought the lunkers, the old soaks, out of the deep pools, which emerged in massive and manic hatches, sometimes for only a few days, perhaps a week. Sometimes the circus occurred on the Beaverkill as early as the first week in June, but sometimes, according to water temperatures no doubt, it was delayed for several weeks. Yes, to fish the Green Drake hatch on the Beaverkill this year with Hawkes, that was an ambition worth the four months of brooding and scheming. To return to the Beaverkill, which I had not fished in ten years, with the old myth himself, yes—it would be Mecca, a vision to hold me throughout another long dry city winter.

But there was no adequate imitation of *Ephemera guttulata*—that was common knowledge. White

Wulffs took a few fish; dyed light-green hackle flies took some; the attempts at exact imitation took very few; and, in the spinner stage, there was the adequate waxy-white and funereal Coffin Fly.

So I experimented that spring, to wile away the wait, and finally, in mid-May, accomplished what to my mind was a major innovation, a contribution to the angling fraternity of staggering proportions. I called it the Pigeon Drake, for the pigeon quill body I had used after a long quill had fluttered down to me, quite mystically, at the very moment I was thinking about this fly one dreary lunch hour. That quill was a portent, and I promptly sent my two older sons out to collect me several dozen in the park at a penny a quill. They brought in ninety-seven, but I used only thirty in my experiments, and ultimately made only four or five usable flies.

The result is hard to describe. It was not a small fly, nor a particularly neat fly. The tip of the quill, through which I had inserted exactly three stems of stripped badger hackle for the tail, had to be strapped firmly to the shank of the #12 hook. Peering up through specially purchased contact lenses from the bottom of a filled bathtub at numerous flies floating there (the door had to be locked to keep out my skeptical wife and distracting children), I observed that the white impala wings of the Wulff flies, sparsely tied, closely resembled the translucent wings of the Green Drake (and many other flies, which perhaps explains part of its extraordinary success). I dyed pure white hackle in green tea. The pigeon quill body, however, is what made the fly: it was natural, translucent, and would cock slightly upward if properly strapped to the shank. Frankly, it was the work of genius, and I could not wait to fish it with Mike and Hawkes on the Beaverkill—Mecca.

But it rained the first three days of my week's vacation, and all I could do was take Brannigan's abuse to the effect that a man who had not been out on the streams *once* by June ninth was a fallen man, fallen indeed, a man given over to mercantilism and paternalism and other such crimes and moral diseases as were destroying the world, or at least a noble sport. "These are dangerous years for you, Nick," he advised me. "Worse will lead to worse."

The fourth day was Brannigan's one day of work, his one day of homage to mercantilism and paternalism, and since Hawkes was not to be heard from (apparently he had disappeared), I went out glumly to a small mountain stream nearby and surprised myself by having a delightful day catching seven-

and eight-inch brookies and browns on tiny #18 and #20 Cahills and Adamses, dry. It was fun watching the spirited streaks of trout shoot out of their cover and gulp the little flies; it was real sport handling them on 6X tippets. But it was not Mecca.

That night I could bear it no longer. Indirections lead to indirections, and I, a mercantilist, had no business being subtle. "Mike," I said, "it's the tenth of June. There have been no reports that the Green Drake hatch has started and it's due momentarily. Don't you have *any* idea where Hawkes is? Can't you simply hunt him up and ask him if he'll go to the Beaverkill with us to-morrow?"

Brannigan roared. "Sure. I know where Hawkes is. But you just don't ask him like that. It takes some engineering, and some luck. He's got to ask you."

"Dammit. What is he, Mike, a saint?"

Mike smiled and sipped at his fourth beer.

"Did you make the damn guy up?"

"All right. All right. I suppose I can find him. But I can't promise a thing."

Two days later, the night before I had to leave, after two days of mediocre fishing in the Esopus, Brannigan said simply, "Hawkes is going tomor-row; said we could come if we want to."

I tried to answer calmly. Though I still didn't

[115]

believe a word about Hawkes, not a word of it, a myth is a myth, and it comes with ineluctable power, a power elusive and haunting.

The next morning at eight o'clock Brannigan was at his garage arranging his tackle, selecting from his six fly rods the best for the day.

"Hawkes thinks there might be a Green Drake hatch this evening," the bright white-haired Irishman said, "but that there might not."

Already a hedge; the tricks of the prophets, the ambiguities of the mediums. He didn't exist. Not the Hawkes I'd dreamed about.

Then, as I got out my gear and piled it beside Brannigan's, Hawkes arrived in his forty-six Dodge. His gaunt, lined face was that of a saint, or of a gunman. His eyes were deep set, limned with shadowy black globes; his fingers were long and thin and obviously arthritic. He walked stiffly toward us.

"Brannigan, old Branny, so this is our young friend," he said, extending his bony hand. "Has he made all the adequate preparations? If he is to be admitted into our little club, he must agree to will his ashes to us, that we may sprinkle them upon the waters of the Beaverkill."

Brannigan tried to suppress a smile. I tried, gently, to remove my hand from Hawkes' firm but friendly grasp.

"The Beaverkill," he continued, looking warmly at me, smiling, "home of Gordon and Darbee and Dettee: Mecca. Tell me, Nick, do you face the Beaverkill every morning and every evening at sunset? Do you pray to the gods?"

"Of course he does, Hawkes," said Mike. "Now let's get started. This will be his only real day of trout fishing for the year."

"Very curious," said Hawkes, shaking his head. "One day of trout fishing. I'm sure our young friend has the burdens of the world upon him, then. Nevertheless, one day of real fishing can be enough. Especially at Mecca. It can be made to serve the whole of the year."

I smiled, an embarrassed, naive smile that spread and spread all day, until my cheeks hurt, on that long unforgettable drive to Mecca.

The drive to the Beaverkill should have taken no more than an hour. It was nine o'clock, and I had all hopes of catching the late-morning rise. But it took about an hour for us merely to pack Hawkes' old Dodge, an immaculate, impeccably ordered vehicle, with each object in its proper place: rods, waders, vest, extra fly boxes, net, and Jack Daniels whisky. There was a holder for his pipe above the dashboard, disposal bags, and four cans of beer neatly packed into the ample glove compartment. Hawkes placed each of our items of equipment carefully into the car, with such measured movements that he might have been giving them permanent homes. As he picked up each piece of tackle he would contemplate it for a moment and then comment on its appropriateness to the sport. "Branny, you know that felt is best for the Beaverkill—and yet you bring hobnails. Curious. Is there a special reason for that, Branny? Do you know something you're not telling? Have reports reached you of great mountains of silt and mud being washed into it? You surely would not be using them simply to impress the pedestrian likes of Nick and me, to taunt us with the fruit of some large sale of flies to a posh New York City tackle shop?"

And then, when the felt waders were brought out from Brannigan's garage, after another five minutes of slow, meticulous scrutiny, "I suppose you know that the glue you've used won't last the day. But the Irish are knowledgeable men, and if you've failed to use the preparation I gave you last winter, I'm sure you have your reasons."

At eleven we set out. Too late for the morning rise, but still early enough for a long day on the river. We wouldn't even have to stop for lunch, I thought, hopefully: pick up a sandwich or two for the vest, and hit the stream as soon as possible. I had a raging fever to be on the stream.

The old Dodge scrunched slowly out of Brannigan's pebbled driveway, made the semicircle onto the tarred road, and started, with incredible slowness, west—to Mecca.

Hawkes opened and closed his long arthritic fingers slowly around the wheel. "This is a day not to be rushed," he said. "It is going to be an experience, an event. It must be savored."

"Come off it, Hawkes," said Brannigan.

Hawkes stopped the car abruptly. Smack in the middle of the highway. Without taking his eyes away from the windshield in front of him, he said, with dead seriousness: "If this is to be a day of cynicism, of doubt, of feverish behavior by an unruly Irishman, I would be glad to turn around, return said Irishman to his own car, and make my peace elsewhere. I have my doubts that the Green Drakes will appear anyway; the temperature dropped to fifty-two degrees night before last— which, I take it, the less sensitive scholars of the streams *did not notice*—the barometer is falling, if slowly, and the moon was not to be seen last night. My fingers are tight, I have a telltale itch along my right thigh, and this *could* become a highly dubious proposition all the way around."

[119]

"Okay, okay, Hawkes. I apologize. Please—
let's go."

"You're tense, man. Sink into the day. Don't
force it. The electricity of such feverish thinking is transmuted imperceptibly but ineluctably to
Mr. Brown Trout. The result you can well guess."

My smile spread, my cheeks ached. Three miles
down the road Hawkes stopped at a gas station, got
out, and asked the attendant about the composition
of the gasoline. Hawkes got a drop on his fingers,
smelled it, touched it gently to his lips, smiled, and
wiped his fingers carefully on some paper towel-
ing. "It is quite possible after all, gentlemen, that
the Green Drake *will* make his appearance this
afternoon. Very curious."

We started out again, and this time Hawkes was
silent, thoughtful, meditative for five minutes.
Several times he stopped the car at small mountain
creeks, got out of the car, scrutinized the water,
threw boysenberries into the eddies, and began to
hum quietly. "Boys," he said, nodding, "it's really
going to be a day. This is going to be an event."

Three more miles down the road, feeling im-
measurably dry, he had to get a small bracer at a
roadside tavern. We each ended having three tall
beers apiece. Another mile, feeling too wet, he had
to relieve himself, and did so in a conspicuously

high arc. Half a mile farther and he stopped abruptly, whistled a long clear whistle, and watched a blonde farmgirl carrying a child walk slowly across a field of knee-high corn shoots. "It is a day of poetry, of cosmic stillness," he informed us. "She is the Madonna agrarianistically developed."

When I noted, unobtrusively, that it was now two-thirty, he advised: "There are lessons to be learned on a day like this. Let it not be rushed; let it be savored. It is a day composed on the celestial lyre. An event. We need only stop at the Blue Goose tavern, my dear Nick, and we will get to Mecca in good time. Branny, where is that oasis?"

Mike did not remember, but several inquiries proved that it was seven miles out of our way, up an unpaved road. No matter. It was impossible to fish the Beaverkill during the Green Drake hatch without first stopping at the Blue Goose. It was a ritual. Part of the sacraments. The Blue Goose was a holy place, a temple pilgrimages were made to.

It looked like a cruddy overaged bar to me. We stayed an hour, but only two miracles occurred: the floor rose three inches on my fourth beer, and I was able to walk out. We took a six-pack with us and were on our way, due west, over the last little mountains, pilgrims, pioneers, seekers of the holy Mecca.

We arrived in Roscoe at five-thirty, still in time for a long evening's fishing, but Hawkes thought we should look up Bishop Harry Darbee before heading for the stream, to seek his blessings as well as his advice. This could not be done directly. It was first necessary to head for the Antrim Lodge, to the cool dark cellar for a few stronger snorts than we'd had. Hawkes invoked us each to empty two double shots of Jack Daniels, which done, he launched into a series of incisive questions of the good bartender. But when that dispenser of firewater said that the water had been high and that a few men had been in that very afternoon with limits they'd taken on spinning rods, Hawkes became violent and Brannigan had to grab his arm, even hold his mouth, as he shouted, "Coffee grinders! Hoodlums! Saracens!"

Darbee was not to be found, but Walt Dette was home, and Hawkes conned him out of a dozen hackles from a natural blue, after an hour of talk about breeding of this rare bird.

At seven o'clock we hit the stream. Not ten miles downriver, where Dette had told us to go, but a spot directly below Junction Pool. One look at the water, after that interminable drive, and I had insisted. Hawkes shrugged. It did not make much difference, he said.

Once parked, Mike and I suited and set up hurriedly. Hawkes sat back and puffed at his pipe. "Long as you two have the Saint Vitus' Dance, you might as well indulge it. Go on. Git, you two. Takes an old man like me a while to get into the proper frame of mind for his holy stream. It is not to be rushed."

We wasted no time. Brannigan headed downstream, I up—and we were flailing away wildly at the waters for a full twenty minutes before Hawkes, on stiff legs, puffing contentedly on his pipe, ambled to the spot on the stream nearest the car. Fish were beginning to rise steadily just at that moment, and the large pale-green duns began to rise in swarms from the water. I switched from a Cahill to a #12 Pale Watery Dun, and then to a White Miller, a White Wulff, and then to an imitation Drake. All in rapid succession. Nothing. Something was missing. My mind was beer-fogged, my casting was sloppy, I was wobbly, and something important was trying to press itself out of my unconscious. Below me, Brannigan, fishing nymphs dead drift, took nothing.

Hawkes waded out a few feet, stood stark still like a crane, fixed his glasses, took the temperature of the water, tested it with his hand, peered long into the swirling duns, the many dimples of rising

fish, and selected a fly from his single aluminum
case. It took him a full minute to affix it, but when
he had he looked at the water again, clipped off the
fly, and started the process again. He pulled the
leader tight, clipped off the end bit, ran the leader
through his mouth six or seven times, and peeled
off line.

I was staggered when his first cast brought a
strike only moments after the fly had alighted.
Deftly he played an eleven-inch brown, drew it
close until it turned belly up, and then neatly
netted it.

The scene was unbelievable. The sun was several feet above the tree line now, and seemed to
hang, luminous and diffused, ready to drop at any
moment. The hatch was fantastic, the large pale-
green drakes thick as locusts, heavy-winged and
fat. Lesiurely two- and even three-pound trout
stalked them, inches beneath the surface. It was
like a slow-motion film. They would cruise, like
sharks, their dorsals extended above the water line,
and heavily suck down the fallen drakes. Everything took place on the surface—methodically,
devastatingly. There must have been fifty trout
cruising in that long flat pool—no doubt, many
were denizens of the large lakelike pool several
hundred yards downstream. They were in no

hurry. For them it was an event, an annual feast some of them had probably partaken of for four or five years. My hands and limbs were shaking.

Hawkes' next cast brought another strike, but it was short and he retrieved the line quietly, without a ruffle of the surface.

I made a full twelve casts before he cast again, and this time the rise to his fly—which I could not see—was not short. While playing what was obviously a two-pound trout or better, he called softly for me to come to his position. I scampered through the water like a water buffalo, convinced that he had both the right spot and the right fly, and scurried to his side just as he netted a fine eighteen-inch brown, broke its neck, and creeled it.

I was frantic. There could not be more than another thirty-five minutes of visibility. Wildly I tried four or five different flies, my back cast slapping the water behind me noisily. Hawkes did not frown. He did not take his eyes from the water. I had never seen such intense concentration.

Then I remembered—*how could I have forgotten?*—and my entire body shook with excitement as I did: the Pigeon Drake.

I was so unhinged that it took five tries before I got the leader through the eye of this miraculous fly, and when I jerked the knot tight the line broke. I tried again and this time managed. The Pigeon Drake hung convincingly from my line.

Carefully I false-cast out fifteen, then twenty feet of line. I felt calm and confident now, as icy and knowledgeable and canny as Hawkes. Then I released the last few feet of line, shot them through the guides, and happily, expectantly, watched the fly drop to the water.

It landed like a shot pigeon. But immediately one of those slow-motion monsters glided portentously toward it. I watched, heart beating wildly, while the dorsal neared. The spotted back of the fine brown and each and every aspect of his awesome body were clear to me as he moved, inches below the surface. Then he stopped, the fly not four inches from his nose. The trout was motionless, but not tense. "Take it. Take it, you old soak," I whispered. I twitted the fly. "Take it," I murmured again. Once more I twitched the fly, and this time the movement did it. When the reverberations in the water ceased, the fly began to sink, like the City in the Sea, majestically down. Unmistakably, the trout turned its nose up. It did. I'll swear to it. And then, with noble calm it glided toward a nearby natural, and took it. It had been a sneer—the sophisticated sneer of a wiseacre trout if I'd ever seen one. And it finished me. Dejectedly I retrieved my line, clipped off the fly, dropped it into the water (where it promptly sank like a stone), reeled in my line, and dismantled my rod.

In the remaining half hour of visibility Hawkes calmly took three more fish, the largest a full twenty inches, minutes before darkness set in.

The drive home, after Hawkes had finished three almost raw hamburgers and two cups of black coffee, took exactly sixty-two minutes. Hawkes did not particularly race along the road.

All the way back I had visions of those swarms of greenish duns rising from the flat pool, fluttering clumsily, falling back, drifting downstream, and being leisurely sharked down by slow-motion monsters. Brannigan had caught nothing; I had caught nothing; three anglers we met had taken one small trout among them; innumerable trout-fishers throughout the East take nothing during the massive Green Drake hatches; but Hawkes had taken six in about an hour, using no more than several dozen casts. Alas, I can only further the myth about Hawkes: I certainly cannot disprove it.

He evaded all our questions for the first forty-five minutes of that quick drive home with a skill to dwarf Falstaff's.

"Yes, it did seem like the Green Drake, *Ephemera guttulata Pictet,* was the major hatch."

"You're not saying they weren't taking those duns, are you?" asked Mike pointedly. "I saw them take a dozen myself."

"Exactly what were you using?" I asked.

"How, how, how! An extraordinary question. Not at all an easy question to answer, my dear Nick. There are a dozen subtle factors involved that . . ."

"Come off it, Hawkes," said Brannigan.

". . . that the unenlightened Irishmen who slash the streams—and whom it has been my misfortune to fall in with during my decline—would scarcely understand. Brannigan, Branny old boy, did you see the innocence, the absolute simplicity of that farm-girl holding her child this afternoon? The Madonna —no less."

"Will you simply tell us what fly you were us-ing?" Mike persisted.

"A question impossible to answer, beyond my power to answer. Ah, but did you see the colors of the sun settling below the tree line, the ochers, the magentas, the great song of the heavens? You must scatter my ashes there, Branny. It is so written."

We were silent while he dropped us off at Brannigan's house, carefully unloading all our tackle—this time without comment. He asked if we'd like a fish apiece (though not the two trophies).

We both said no.

Then he got back into his car stiffly, turned over the motor, looked at us both with those ancient and shadowy eyes, smiled, and said: "It was an event, gentlemen—was it not? We have been to Mecca. And it will last longer than these six trout, which I shall dispatch shortly—the least part of our trip."

"You won't tell us what you took them on?" I asked.

"You've missed the point. Nick," he said, taking my hand in his bony fingers, "until next year . . ."

With that he drove off around Brannigan's graveled circle and up the road. We could see the old Dodge pause on the highway. Hawkes leaned far out of the car, looked up at the moon, and said something loudly that we could not hear.

"Perhaps it *will* last longer," said Mike, putting

his arm around my shoulder and smiling broadly there in the moonlight. I started preparing for the long trip back to the city, for the long year.

"Perhaps," I said.

And it has.

6/Dog-Day Redemptions

Annihilating all that's made
To a green thought in a green shade.
            —ANDREW MARVELL

Large amorphous forms lumbered against the bare brightening of the horizon. Now and then, low guttural sounds emerged from the dark field.

I had risen at four, gotten to the stream less than a half hour later, and had rigged my old Granger and affixed (in the glow from the headlights) a Hair Coachman. Now I was standing beside my old Mercedes, smoking a pipe and waiting the last few moments before light broke sufficiently for me to head through the pasture without tripping over one of the still sleeping cows.

I had encountered several bulls in that field in midday, and did not care to encounter them in the dark.

It had rained the night before and the clouds still hung heavy and low; the sun would not break cleanly. Despite the rain, the late-July morning was warm and humid.

A few moments later I slipped under the wooden cow fence and, staying close to the feeder creek, walked through the mists toward the river. I wore only sneakers, Levi's, a light cotton jacket, and my felt fishing hat, flopped down all the way around. The low guttural moans and the long sweet whistles of the crickets were the only sounds at first. The large forms continued to lumber along the silhouetted slope of the hill. And then I heard the quick, steady, sliding sound of the river.

Summer streams will often shock the fisherman who fishes only in the spring: some are virtually gone, low and unfishable; others, like the West Branch of New York's Au Sable, reach their peak for the fly-fisherman in the summer while earlier they were fast torrents. And still others are metamorphosed into entirely different streams, with new qualities, new mysteries. The contours change, and where before a raging bend defied even weighty sinkers, now it is a modest pool, flecked with inviting foam, each nook and hiding

[132]

place formed by rock or fallen tree visible. Most
eastern streams have dropped several feet, and I
know sections which in the spring were flat rushing water that become spotted with innumerable
protruding rocks, engineering attractive glides and
runs and pockets. Where wading may have been
impossible or treacherous, in the summer it frequently becomes genial. On the less popular streams,
you may well find yourself pleasantly alone.

I had a private river that morning—shared only
with the cows, which at various moments came
down to the water's edge and, munching, observed
me.

Morning is the best time for summer angling.
The water and air are usually coolest then, and
the fish most active. I heard fish rising when I
reached the river, and the sight that greeted me,
before five, was extraordinary. In the soundless
swirling mists of that humid morning, before the
sun had crested the Berkshire foothills, the stream
was pocketed with rising trout. In the eddies and
riffles and flat water, the stream virtually boiled.

It was not a defined rise, such as you may see in
May or early June; the Quill Gordon, the Hendrickson, the Cahill, and Green Drake have all come
in their good time—and departed. Several minor

varieties of stream life were coming off the water, and some of the fish were tailing for nymphs while others slurped on the surface.

I tried the Coachman first and on the third cast took a modest brown under ten inches and decided to kill it. His stomach was a book. There were a minnow, several terrestrials, an undigested moth, and a small mass of green nymphs. I fished alone for five hours that morning, and all along the stream fish were feeding steadily. It was pleasant work, wading upstream in my sneakers and jeans, growing hot as the day grew hot and then splashing my face with the cooler water. I kept one more, a twelve-incher that fell to a Muddler Minnow fished dry and twitched under an overhanging maple branch—and caught five or six others. At about ten most of the visible feeding stopped, except for the slap-rise of dace and sunfish, and I headed home. It had, by brunch-time, been a full day.

I especially like to fish several small crystalline creeks in the summer, tramping them in my sneakers and rough trousers, following them high into the hills. Often they are spring-fed and remain cold enough to keep the trout quick and about their business, not burrowing under rocks during the dog-days of summer. These little streams are like private beats for me and I rarely meet anyone along them, though they are often heavily fished in the spring.

Jassids are good here, a tiny #18 or #20 Spent-wing Adams, a small Muddler Minnow now and then in August, and the inexhaustible Hair-wing Royal Coachman, in a #18, sparsely tied and with a Golden Pheasant tippet tail rather than brown or white impala hair. I fish them upstream, flicking my fly on a short line into the pockets and riffles. I like to dye my tippets a red-brown with Tintex, for this is delicate work; 7X is not too fine. The fish are rarely large—often enough under nine inches—but some are natives, and the occasional twelve-incher can make you tremble when it breaks the surface of one of those small pools or riffles and fights out into all its corners.

I never keep fish from such streams. Why defeat the stream? Why defeat myself? It is enough to slip back away from the towns, following the turns and rock-strewn paths of the creek, hopping here and there like a gigantic grasshopper, poking stealthily into a long gin-clear run over slate that has four or five little brookies flouncing under that low hemlock. The tiny Hair Coachman flicks upstream and hooks left and drops silently several feet above them; I see every gesture and turn and lithe movement of the brookies. The fly drifts down over them; one turns and rises, a slow, languid, steady rise, but then arcs back. I try another cast, but it is too loud and they spook and disappear.

So I sit on a bone-dry rock in mid-creek, take out my pipe, clean it, pack it with good tobacco, puff it slowly, and watch a kingfisher, a couple of swallows, a bright bluejay high in the hemlock.

A half hour later I try them again. This time, though, I go upstream—circuitously, with impeccable care—and cast down with a slack line so that I can place the fly closer to the little riffle near that opposite bank, so that the sun is in front of me. I am working with a short line and can manage it all without drag, but there's only one or possibly two chances and then I will spook them again.

It works. A little brookie rises to the Spent-wing Adams without hesitation, flips and flops, and then gets beached, palmed under the belly, unhooked, and sent home.

One such spring-fed mountain creek flowed out of the hills and then down into a town in which I once spent several months with my family. We used to lunch sometimes at a coffee shop whose screened porch hung out over a picturesque little pool. Naturally I always sat in the corner, so I could get a good look at the stream. There was a small riffle at the pinched neck of the pool and a large boulder along the bank directly beneath me, forming the right bank if one were looking up-stream.

One day, I saw a genuinely considerable trout on the lip of the slight summer current, below the alder shoots; it was spotted umber and fanning his broad fantail as he turned in a half arc. A nymph must have risen, for the white hooked jaw spread as he turned, tailed, and then returned out of sight to his riffled place beneath the boulder. My heart pounded: the trout was a full eighteen inches, and in that small pool he was a whale. I watched him several times. Except in the deepest corner, under the rock, his dorsal would stand above the water, making him an unwilling amphib-ian as the current wagged its spare August lines.

Several days later I tried for him, tried to tease out this extraordinary anachronism in the small stream, this last of the titans. I did not think I would kill him; I knew I would not kill him. Per-haps I could carry him twenty yards downstream and slip him over the falls, into the deeper pools. I did want to catch him.

I crept gingerly along the rocks in sneakers;

there was no need to wade and any movement in
the pool would have spooked him. Then, some
thirty feet downstream, I sent my line sweeping
back and forth, taking tack with the flight of swallows that shot down the stream's alley. My cast
fell short and did not hook to the right, under the
boulder. I let the fly come all the way back to me
in a natural float over dead water, though, and then
began again.

This time my cast was perfect. The fly landed
high up into the neck of the pool and far over
toward the right bank. The fly scooted zig-zag in
the little current and then, suddenly, *whomp*,
the fish took it. I struck too sharply. The fly stayed
with him and the bare leader zipped up out of the
water and dropped in front of me.

As the hot arid days of August continued, I'd
try for that fish early in the morning, in mid-after-
noon, in the evening, whenever I had a spare half
hour. I raised him twice more and both times
snapped him off. When I tried a 5X leader, he
would have none of me and wouldn't even sniff
up at my offerings.

And all those weeks, whenever we went out to
lunch, it was always to that coffee shop. And the
trout remained trapped in his little pool.

Then, several days before we were to leave, I

took several hours and determined to have it out with him. I'd dyed my leaders carefully, checked hook points, prepared a select group of tiny flies. I made my approach with great care and was readying my first cast when I discovered I was not alone. A bit above the little pool stood a young man of sixteen or seventeen, his dungarees rolled up to his knees, a frog spear in his right hand.

He sneered at my elaborate equipment and watched, shaking his head, as I worked my way slowly toward the pool. When he saw where I was going to fish, he shouted: "Nothin' in there, mister. Nothin' but water. And not much of that."

I smiled and thought of leaving. I did not particularly want this young man to know about my leviathan.

"Maybe a couple dace or suckers. You need all that equipment for dace, mister?"

"Keep quiet for five minutes and I'll show you what's in there," I said in a loud whisper. "There's a huge trout up under that boulder."

"Haw-haw," the boy laughed loudly.

I told him to get up on the ledge where he could see, and for God's sake to keep his big mouth shut. He shook his head but went up to the perch I had designated and sat there cross-legged and skeptical.

On my third cast I turned him over. The fish took the fly solidly and immediately skyrocketed up into the air. He was a magnificent brown, his jaw already hooked, his body sleek and long. I held my rod high, gave him line as he burrowed under the boulder, and tried to catch my breath. He sulked for a moment and I made no effort to rouse him: I needed the rest as much as he did.

"Wow!" cried the young frog-spearer. "That's a tre-mendous fish, mister. Want me to spear him for ya?"

"No! Stay where you are! Don't come near him!"

The boy stayed put.

The trout did not. He began to thrash wildly around the little pool, scurrying frantically up along the rocks where his dorsal would stick a full inch above the surface, rolling and turning, sending the water into a froth as he went into a flurry of spirited tumbles. And then, suddenly, he was off: the leader had caught in the vortex of several rocks and neatly parted.

"Haw-haw!" laughed the boy. "Knew you'd never ketch him on the pretty little rod. Bet you coulda caught him with a spinning rod; bet you could snare him, force him into a net, stone him, even; spear him, maybe."

I said softly, as I reeled in the slack line, that I did not catch trout that way. Not anymore.

"Haw. Bet you plain don't ketch 'em," he said. "Period, mister."

That seemed to end our conversation and I knew I would not raise him again, so I left the stream without a word.

When I saw the fish from the coffee-shop porch the next afternoon, I noticed something new: a long white scar on his back. I decided not to try for him again.

That night and for all the next day it poured wildly. And then, the day we left, when the waters had cleared, I searched for him again—watched from the porch, then went down to the stream without my rod and scanned the waters closely. He was gone.

Whether the boy got him with his spear or with a stone or with a net, or whether he went off with the rains, I simply do not know. I only know that trapped trout remains deep inside me. As many other uncaught trout do.

One late-August day, when the sun had begun to bank behind the looming Catskills and the air to grow cool, I was working my way slowly up a long flat run when I found myself seventy yards behind a superb and meticulous fly-fisher. He was half hidden along the left bank and working a small pocket behind an overturned tree. His casts were deft and economical, with a minimum of false casting, and in short order he had taken three solid browns and gently released each of them downstream of where he was fishing. After this he carefully waded ashore and disappeared into the streamside trees.

I thought he had gone upstream, or off-stream, so I waited a few moments and then began to work slowly up into his area.

Fishing the same pool he had left a half hour earlier, I slow-struck two splash rises and then took a nice eleven-inch brown on a skittered spider and released it; then I headed for the bank.

The man was sitting with his back to a tree, smoking a hooked pipe; he had obviously been watching me and nodded with a quiet approval that I did not deserve. He was not much older than myself.

"I see you don't kill them either," he said.

"I take a few now and then," I admitted readily. "But I do put back most of them. Especially on a little-fished stream like this. It's almost like a club."

"Yes," he said. "I found this place about four

years ago and rarely meet anyone when I begin to fish it in July. Which is much of what it's all about, isn't it? Coming a bit closer to the laws under the surface—the stream's as well as your own. Plying a gentle art that has no justification beyond itself."

I nodded.

"Sit down for a bit," he said, "and have your pipe. I liked the way you worked the spider. That'll ruffle them up sometimes on a muggy summer's day, won't it?"

I sat down with my back against a nearby oak and we talked quietly for a half hour or so, exchanging lore about the stream. He was exceptionally knowledgeable about this summer angling and told me this particular run was a fine spot for terrestrials of a wide variety; he pointed to the canopy of oak, maple, and locust branches that domed the few hundred yards, and to the few dozen cows that wandered the banks upstream, in the meadow. He explained how they carried certain land flies into the stream, how others dropped from the thick branches, and how the whole area grew exceptionally buggy in mid-summer. He told me how two or three really large browns would move up into the run from the deeper pools downstream, usually in the early evening, and how he'd turned one over early that

[143]

day and had caught one at four-o'clock one morning a number of weeks earlier on a #16 Ginger Bivisible.

After we'd talked for a while, exchanged some tobacco and a few intimate comments about work and family, he suddenly broke a short pause by asking: "Did you ever kill a great number of trout?"

The question was abrupt and I looked carefully at him for a moment before answering. Then I told him that I had, usually on Opening Days, taken my limit a good number of years running, and that in the spring when I was in my teens I kept a limit whenever I could. He asked if I knew why I'd killed so many and I told him frankly that it was probably because of the power of display when I returned and sometimes because of the competition when I'd fished with others.

He nodded and then asked if I usually fished alone now; I said I did. Was there any other reason why I'd killed a lot, he asked. I thought for a moment and then suggested that there might have been some kind of vicarious thrill in the killing.

"Perhaps," he said.

"But there's really more to it, isn't there?" I asked.

"Yes," he said. "There usually is."

"Did *you* ever . . . kill a good number?" I asked.

"Yes. Like you, when I was young, I took as many as I could get. And then once, twenty-odd years ago . . . that was the last time."

"Do you want to tell me about it?" I asked.

He got up, walked to the stream bank, and pointed at a trout's dorsal showing in shallow water near the opposite bank. Then he turned and came back and sat down again. He began pressing fresh tobacco into his pipe, looked at me, and then said, "Well, if you've another half hour, I don't mind telling you."

I nodded, yes, I had time, but said nothing.

"It was shortly after I left the Army," he began. "Those few years had been constrained but neatly ordered, and I was much at ends—not knowing whether to enter my father's business or break off on my own, in perhaps an entirely different field. Not an unusual or particularly profound situation, but at the time, seeing a lifetime stretched out in front of me, it meant a lot."

I told him that the situation was familiar to me.

"I was starved for something," he continued. "Perhaps my schooling hadn't really touched what was important in me; perhaps it was too professional and narrow; perhaps it had been simply bland. I was curious and restless, anxious to do something important but without any assurance that there was something important in me. I wanted excitement—and peace; I wanted to risk everything for some cause of value. And perhaps it was simply that 'Youth to itself rebels, though none else near.' "

He paused for a moment, picked up his fine Orvis rod from the grass, flexed it, and then lay it down again carefully.

"I tried a few odd jobs, earned a few hundred dollars, and then decided to buy an old Ford and head across country. I had broken with most of my old friends; I saw no one; and I had become something of a recluse, reading a lot for the first time—all sorts of books, with no pattern, only raw hunger. Somehow fishing had always been important to me—not as a profession but something that brought a degree of absorption. I took my spinning rods and a box of tackle and took off by myself. It was August, and hot as a skillet."

"Didn't you fly-fish, then?" I asked.

"Not then. It was very curious. I wasn't going anywhere and yet I was going there in one terrible rush. I aimed my little black car along the thruways and speedways in that scorching late summer and drove fifteen or sixteen hours a day—straight and a lot too fast, a lot too intensely. My hands gripped the wheel fiercely and I saw nothing but that white snake of a highway in front of me and the other speeding cars. At night I'd simply pull over and sleep for a few hours in the back of the little car.

"On the third day, though, I began to move out of the Midwest and into the Black Hills of South Dakota. Even the billboards and the tourist traps could not kill the spectacular yellows and greens, the new forms and shapes of an elemental world beneath the garishness man had built. I wanted to stop. I wanted very much to stop. But the car kept rocketing along through all of this new world —but never a part of it. I went through the Dakotas and then through Wyoming and into the Yellowstone area. Am I boring you?"

He asked this with genuine concern.

"I promised you a fishing story and I'm afraid I've become quite autobiographical."

"Isn't every fishing story autobiographical?" I asked.

"Yes. *Style est l'homme*—even on the stream." He smiled and then, when I motioned with my hands that he should continue, went on. "In West Yellowstone I noticed a few fishermen standing by a station wagon, their rods propped against it, a few decent trout lying on newspaper on the dropped rear door. I wanted to talk to them; I felt a kind of connection to them. But I could not bring myself to say a word.

"While having a bite, I remembered a lake a fishing friend who summered in Idaho had once told me about. What was the name? Big Little Lost Lake. Yes, that was it. It had, he'd said, lunkers in it. But where in Idaho? I went into the nearest tackle shop, where I felt immediately at home, and marveled at several huge trout that adorned the walls. They were larger by far than any I'd seen in our eastern streams: four- and five-pound browns, a three-pound brookie, and a seven-pound cutthroat. I looked over the tackle and started up a tentative conversation with one of the salesmen, a pleasant, weathered man in a plaid shirt who obviously knew his angling well. He seemed disappointed, though, when I told him I did no fly-fishing, and said that the spinning rod was doing its best to ruin a number of fine Montana streams. He was quite frank in admitting that he thought fly-only sections ought to be established on a number of sections. This was twenty years ago. Then I asked him if he'd heard of Big Little Lost Lake and he said no, but that there were hundreds of small and highly productive lakes in

Idaho that he knew nothing about. He got out a number of maps and spread them on a large table. On the first, a fairly small state-wide map, we could find no sign of the lake, but on one of the detailed geodetic maps he spotted a small lake of that name. We transposed the location to the map of the state and saw that it was about one hundred miles away, in a mountainous section he had never fished.

Somehow the name and isolation of that lake had begun to catch my imagination. After buying a few attractive lures I thanked the man, and that very afternoon headed off into Idaho.

"It was dark when I got there three and a half hours later and the moon was only a sliver—not enough to see much by. So I simply pulled over to the side and slept in the car again.

"When I awoke, about six, the lake was veiled with slowly rising mists. It was a small lake, perhaps two miles around, and in a desolate and dreary sagebrush flat. The water was a curious green, a thick green, almost as opaque as pea soup. I was disappointed. I had expected exquisite scenery and crystal-blue water. Had I gotten the wrong lake? Had the lake turned over? Had my friend been fibbing? That's not unknown among fishermen, you know."

"It comes with the territory," I said.

"Toward the far side of the lake," he went on, "I saw a few cabins and headed along the narrow dusty dirt road toward them. The rustic cabins were circled around a little cove, perhaps a hundred yards across, and there were three men fishing from the shore, each with a fly rod. As I stopped the car one of them suddenly got a strike and his rod went into a sudden and pronounced arc. He fought the fish without a sound for a full fifteen minutes and then landed a beautiful trout whose coloring I did not recognize; it was about eight pounds, I guess.

"Without touching the fish, he disengaged the little fly while it flopped in the large boat net, and then he turned the net out carefully into the water. The trout disappeared into that opaque pea-green water almost immediately. My whole body began to shake. I'd never imagined trout really came that size—or that someone could catch such a fish and release him with such lack of emotion.

" 'Looked like a nice one, Pete,' one of the men said.

" 'Not bad. Seven, maybe eight pounds, I guess. Not nearly the size of that rainbow you took last night.'

[150]

"I was astounded. It was a bonanza. I quickly found the proprietor, bought a non-resident license, and secured a small cabin for myself at a nominal price. It felt good to stop here. It felt like a place I had been secretly looking for. I was *grateful* for the place. Do you understand that?

"I went in, bathed, shaved, bought a Coke at the proprietor's little store, and then went back to rest for an hour. My body was tired and throbbing and, I assured myself, there was no need to rush anymore. I was pleased to be at Big Little Lost Lake and there was no need to rush anymore. Perhaps I would find what I was searching for—now that I could stop rushing.

"I slept for about seven hours and woke at eight, just before dusk. I went down to the lake quickly with my spinning rod and saw there the same few men, along with several wives in beach chairs and a few newcomers. Two men with fly rods were hooked up to good fish.

"I began to cast rapidly with a small spoon and then retrieve rapidly. My whole body was braced for action—but I got nothing. Neither did any of the others who were using spinning rods. The fly-rodders caught several apiece that evening, before dark, and kept one each.

[151]

"I returned to my cabin despondent. I had no fly rod and obviously that was what was needed. Besides, I could barely cast with the long rod.

"The next morning I was casting my spoons into that strange cove at daybreak. No one else was there and I experimented by using a dozen different retrieves. None worked. Finally, growing irritated and impatient, I began to fling the spoon out as far as I could. After one such cast, my line became tangled in the gears and since there was so much out I let the lure fall to the bottom—sure I would lose it—while I unsnarled the line. It took me a full fifteen minutes to free it, and even then I had to break off a little knotted loop and retie the line with a small blood knot. Finally I'd done it and with a few light touches, to disengage the lure from a possible snag, began to reel in with sharp, almost hostile, jerks.

"On the third whip of the rod there was a powerful strike and I knew I was into a very large fish, larger than I'd ever hooked. I fought him for a full twenty minutes, during which time he took considerable line from the drag. But a good drag is lethal and finally I brought him close and beached him. He was a full eight pounds—silvery bright and still flapping; he was a hybrid, I later learned, a cutthroat-rainbow. Though he was well up on the shore, I was shaking and afraid he would wriggle free, so I grasped his head firmly with my right hand and drew it back with a sharp *knuck*, scratching a few fingers so that they bled and my blood mingled with the blood that spurted from the break at the trout's neck. I took eight that morning, each time letting the lure sink to the bottom and then retrieving it with short, sharp, almost violent jerks. Two were foul-hooked in the dorsal area. I kept two more, which made my limit of three, and left about one o'clock to have lunch in town. My wrists ached but I was exhilarated.

"That night about five o'clock I went down to the cove again. Six men from a nearby lumber camp had come over and began to fish near me. They had a huge tub filled with ice and beer cans and had already been drinking. They were using rather cheap spin-casting outfits, short and stubby rods with heavy line. In a few moments I caught a nice four-pounder and reluctantly released it. Ten minutes later I took another and released it, too. And soon afterward I had a really good one on and was fighting him with pleasure when one of the men came over and whispered hoarsely in my ear, 'Can we have him, mister?'

" 'Sure,' I said, and when I finally got him in I

broke his head back with a *knuck* and threw the fish into their tub. I showed the men what lure I was using and suggested they let it go to the bottom. Perhaps they were impatient—I didn't notice—but only one of them took a fish that night.

"I took another, brought it in rapidly, and *knuck*, broke its neck and threw it in with the first. Then another, *knuck*, and another, *knuck*—happy with their murmurs of praise, happy to be scoring so well. The dusk came on as the sun dropped below the sagebrush hills, and I took another, *knuck*, and another and another—none under two pounds, several near nine. Then it was nearly dark and I was still catching them, some in the dorsal, some in the mouth, one in the tail, and bringing them in rapidly and breaking their necks, *knuck*, *knuck*, *knuck*, like that, and tossing them into the tub until finally I was bone tired and it was nine o'clock and the law said we had to stop.

"One of the men lit a kerosene lamp and I walked up to the tub with him. The others were marveling at my catch and full of congratulations for me.

" 'Gawd, that was something to see,' one of them said.

" 'That guy has a touch like I've never seen.'

[154]

" 'Mister, you're deadly; you're absolutely lethal on trout—you know that?

"And then I saw it: in the glow of the kerosene lamp I saw the tub filled with those huge trout, enough to make limits for all of them. The fish were curved around each other, their bright bodies muted and dirt-flecked. There was blood all over. On my shirt, on my pants, all over the tub. I glanced briefly at the pile of trout corpses I'd made —they might as well have been people—and without saying a word to the men walked to my cabin, busted my spinning rod on my knee, and began to cry."

The man smiled quietly at me, drew once or twice deeply on his cold pipe, and then knocked out the ashes.

"Even my face was filled with blood, I saw when I looked at myself in the mirror. And when I lit up the fire in the cast-iron stove, my hands glowed red in the orange light."

"That's an extraordinary story," I told him. I stood and then walked over to him and touched his shoulder.

"Oh, I suppose some people have killed more. I suppose killing fish is a thing some people do all their lives. I didn't feel guilty about it, you know . . ."

"I know."

"It wasn't the trout really. People have killed more. I used to think that if the gods were truly forgiving, we were each entitled to one such slaughter: it bleeds the imagination of impurities. But then I read where they've dropped barb wire in that cove, which has springs that attract hordes of trout for several weeks in August; the water, the pea-green water, is crammed with vegetable and animal life, which is why the fish grow so big. Yes, they've put restrictions on that cove: I've seen them in the game laws. And I might have done some permanent damage there in restricting what was real sport for some good people. That troubles me. We can't afford to lose many more good trout waters, you know. Not because people have un-exorcized demons in them. No need to take it out on the fish. It's as unworthy of them as it is of us."

"You seem to have worked your demons out," I said quietly.

"I was lucky," he said. "And I worked at it."

We talked for a few more moments and then he said he thought he'd try the upper end of the long run, if I didn't mind, and when I said of course I didn't, he shook hands with me firmly, nodded, and walked slowly upstream.

I sat for a half hour and watched him deftly flick

his line back and forth as the sun dropped and then angled through the heavy canopy of trees, prismatic and jeweled. He took another trout, then another, and released each carefully. Without turning back to me, he worked his way methodically upstream and was out of sight.

I got into the water and fished halfheartedly for ten or fifteen minutes without raising a fish. There was a good brown in a fixed feeding position below an upturned tree root, but I decided to save him for another summer's day.

I've fished that stream a couple of dozen times since then but have never again met my friend. I don't even know his name.

7/Autumn Trouting

Where are the songs of Spring? Ay, where
are they?
Think not of them, thou hast thy music
too,—

—JOHN KEATS, "To Autumn"

In August the multitudes turn to the beaches by hordes, the politicians turn to their conventions and their drums and flags and slogans, most of the sporting magazines turn to hunting, the city turns deathly gray and dry and hot and anxious, and I begin to hear the last chords of the fly-fisherman's year.

August wanes and the last dog days slip, in early September, into mixtures of cool mornings and warm, bright afternoons; the corn ripens and is drawn from the sides of stalks; the evenings turn cool and the sun drops earlier; and by mid-month there is a definite break and we have come to the last of it.

At noon I come to the stream: it is no longer necessary to beat the sun, but pleasant to linger with it. There is not the avid quality of spring. I have caught some trout this year or I have not caught some trout. September is not full of the expectancy of spring but is languid and self-contained—demanding little, giving everything in its deliberate, melancholic way. It is a time to learn a quiet attentiveness: to allow the water to disclose still more of its mysteries.

The color of the stream has changed, with September rains, to an auburn. The rivers are regaining their size and swoop after the lowness of summer; they grow plump and ample again, and gain back their own, filling the hollowed banks they engrave each spring. The trout begin to leave their cover and roam the heads and skirts of pools: you can see them rise here and then there, sporadically, under the low willow that nearly kisses the stream, in mid-water, along the far bank.

A few flies come off the water—little gray-blue flies, brown flies, a cahill or two, nondescript little stream life. A grasshopper takes a bad leap and flops, struggling, into a long flat run. I watch him travel three feet, a couple of yards, and then he disappears in a swirl. Whether a trout got him or a bass or a sunfish, I cannot tell.

I have brought my terrestrials, my large Adamses, some spiders, some variants, a few bivisibles, and a variety of hair flies—all dry. Perhaps a streamer would score more; perhaps, with little moving on the surface with much regularity, I should try wets. But I have all afternoon, a lovely afternoon, and I'd as well take them my way, on the top, or not at all. I am a little lazy and luxurious and content to fish upstream and watch the cocked fly travel briskly along the surface.

The stream has not been stocked for several months, and whatever is there will be a bit larger, a bit wiser. There will perhaps be fewer of them, but they will be worth my while.

The entire rhythm of the day is different: I come late and leave early; I linger for a few hours and watch a pool, observe the colors of the sumacs, birches, oaks, and willows; I try a bit here and a bit there. There is no hurry. No. There is absolutely no hurry. The whole music of the autumn stream is weighty and slow. There is no anxiousness lest something be missed, lest the big hatch come and be gone without your presence, without that exact and proper fly being discovered at the exact and proper time. Even rain will not spoil it. The season has been fulfilled; it is complete; it is brushed only lightly by melancholy.

I fish perhaps three days each September, though I wish it were more. I fish in early September, when, some years, there is barely any distinction from the warmer dog days of August, except for cooler water in the mornings, an earlier sunset.

Then, perhaps in mid-September, I will slip away alone for a few hours, to watch the change, to record the difference, to take a leisurely drink of the streams as my work begins to accumulate—to re-collect myself, prepare myself for the long year.

In some streams big lake-run rainbows are already making their move. If there has been a heavy storm or two, this is especially likely. One swirls at my Grizzly Wulff, hollowing the flat surface for a moment, but rises short. It is good to know he is there, though I fish over him for another hour without a strike.

By now the trees have made several bold strokes: yellow willow leaves ride the quick surface of the stream; a patch of red-orange oaks flames out of the hillside; the white ash is blue-bronze; a cluster of low dull-purple and crimson sumacs is worth stopping beside. The irritants are gone—the gnats, the no-see-ums, the freezing fingers of Opening Day—and there is only the pleasant purpose of eye and hand.

Then, abruptly, changing luxury to drama, I spot a good trout in mid-water. He is lolling near the surface, nose upstream, looking and gliding here and there. He is not large enough to be exceptional—perhaps thirteen inches—but he is there and ample, spotted and umber in the stream's world, sleek and obviously hungry.

I become absolutely still. The sounds of cricket and katydid and wind swell; the shadows flicker across the stream; and without moving my feet I strain my head through the streamside brush for more strenuous spying.

He is feeding. No. He is wolfing anything that moves under or on top. And there's another, somewhat smaller, beneath the low willow, and another still, downstream, near that angular rock. An indiscriminate feed. No doubt about it: they are beginning the prespawning splurge.

But how to take that thirteen-incher.

The water is a full four feet to the banks, along the entire run, and the brush has grown heavily directly to the shore line. That one trout will be enough; he will amply make the day.

Foxy fishing, cagy fishing—that's what's called for. I watch him a while: there is something to be learned here, in his movements, in his disposition. I will not soon find another lolling so conspicuously near the surface. I watch the way he returns to the same feeding position in mid-stream, how comfortable he seems at that particular spot (but why?), his head moving slightly from side to side, the length of him a fluid wavering auburn line. I watch the way the water sucks down when he takes a surface insect, and how it swishes when he tails for something lower. I watch what he is taking: it's mostly tiny and barely visible, but perhaps he took one of those curious gray-blue flies that time, perhaps a terrestrial when he darted under the low bough of the hemlock. I watch how he moves, with such swift purpose; how far he will dart in one concerted movement; how he turns on his tail—it must have been by sound— and is after that insect behind him. Yes. There is something to be learned here. And there is no hurry.

I slowly work myself into the thinnest brush where I will still be able to get at him. It will be a short roll cast of twenty-five feet; nothing else will do it unless I go way above him, in that shallow stretch, and float down a nymph. No, this is the way he must be taken—if at all.

Gently I slip the rod through the branches now

and strip out line until three or four yards hang over the steep bank.

How to do it?

There may only be one good cast possible, for he is in a kind of hypnotic state and that might snap if I try him clumsily. I need one roll cast to get the line out, another to place it before him. But even then, should the cast go over and above him, upstream? To the side and, with luck, a little hooked to the left? That would be the best—but can I hook with a roll cast? Me? Probably not.

What then?

Finally I decide: the false roll cast must be downstream and away from him; then the next below and behind him, several inches below his tail. Hadn't he turned, (by sound?) a few minutes earlier?

The sun is slanting below the Berkshire foothills now, the shadows are beginning to creep across the surface of the stream. A brief fresh wind scuttles through the brush, dropping a few more oblong yellow willow leaves onto the gliding water.

Now.

The false cast is fine, and I turn slightly and roll out the true cast deftly. The variant lands four, maybe five inches behind the brown. It could have

[164]

been closer, and it is a bit loud. But almost before it lands, the trout turns in a semicircle with his lithe body and without pausing gobbles the fly. It is all in a rush and I strike lightly.

He gives a spirited account of himself and is only a little tired when I release him a few moments later.

The season closed the next Sunday and I returned to that same stream with Paul, driving up in the late morning. We were to meet Sandy at two o'clock, show him a few new runs I had discovered, and close out another season together with a few hours of pleasant afternoon work.

"We don't have much time alone," said Paul as we drove, "away from the little kids."

No, I admitted. And this was a special delight.

"Do you think we'll get some big ones, Dad?" he asked.

"Sometimes the last few days of the season are very good," I said. "There aren't as many fish, but they're a few inches larger, and usually as hungry as a ten-year-old."

"I'm not hungry at all, Dad. I don't want to stop now. I want to get to the stream just as soon as we can. Is Sandy a good fisherman?"

"Excellent," I said. "He's fished a great deal in

Montana. He's caught some tremendous trout—but he doesn't keep any of them."

"Are we going to keep any?" he asked.

"Perhaps a few. Let's see how many we get."

"Do you know any poems about fishing, Dad?"

"A few. There's one by Yeats called 'The Fisherman.' "

"I know that one," said Paul. "But there's not much fishing in it, is there?"

"Not fishing itself; but something that suggests fishing might make a man a better person."

"I don't really understand that poem. I like lots of poems by Yeats, especially 'The Lake Isle of Innisfree' and that one about O'Leary's noble head and Standish O'Grady walking around drunk between the tables and saying silly things—that's a fine one. But sometimes he says a lot of things I don't understand."

"Well, it's not too good to say everything so easy that everyone understands it right away, is it? There's no mystery about it that way. You'd get tired of the poems pretty quick if they were too easy. That would be like a stream where you couldn't help but catch trout every time you threw in your line."

"I'd like that!"

"Well, once or twice it's nice to find a stream

like that, I suppose. But——" I meant to tell him the classic story by Skues about the chap who spent an eternity in hell, forced to catch trout after trout under ideal circumstances. But I was not up to discussing the afterlife this lovely afternoon.

"I wrote a few poems about fishing," said Paul.

"I know. I like them very much."

"Shall I say them?"

"Of course. Why don't you say all the poems you know. This traffic is going to hold us up for an hour."

So Paul recited a dozen or so poems, including several of his own, about "the quick salmon and the lovely trout," and a trout whose teeth looked vicious but who later tasted "just delicious," and one in which "in every nook and every crook" of every stream he'd ever seen there was a trout "that swims all about." Then he asked me if I had ever written one about fishing and I told him about one called "Trouting," in which the trout catches the trouter—which he liked—and another called "The Willowemoc" that I was still "stitching and un-stitching." He insisted that I recite it for him, and I did.

> Sounds enter me, polyphony of wind
> against alder, birch, and water,

its harried rushes riffled, tangled
in the nub of me, delicately.
It is the Willowemoc, famous and known,
that creeps languidly into the eddy
of my soul. It is a river, old,
under burnished alders auburn, gold,
flowing cold and crystal,
prismatic like a redwing's glide,
that helps me to be more—
that in its shock of stillness
feels me, holds me:
Willowemoc.

Paul said it was a pretty good poem, but that it didn't have much about trout fishing in it, nor much rhyme. He said he liked poems that had lots of rhymes in them, real tongue-twisters like Tolkien wrote.

"Did you write that when you were on the Willowemoc?" he asked.

"No, I wrote it at home," I told him. "And to be very honest with you, Paul, I wasn't thinking about the Willowemoc when I wrote it. But the Beaverkill."

"Then why did you lie?"

"Well, I suppose I liked the sound of Willowemoc better. It sounds a little like the tree and . . ."

"But Beaverkill sounds like the animal. I know all about beavers."

". . . and I suppose I rather wanted a stream that would rhyme with 'shock,' because I sort of started with that phrase 'shock of stillness' in my mind."

"Is that fair, Dad? I mean, are you allowed to lie like that when you write a poem? And start from the end? I always start from the beginning."

"Your friend Yeats always complained about the poems of poets who didn't lie enough."

"Did Yeats lie?"

"In a certain way all poets lie. They make up, they switch, they imagine. Hemingway once wrote a story called 'Big Two-Hearted River' and it was all about a fishing trip a boy named Nick took in Upper Michigan. I always thought the name of the stream was made up: it didn't sound like a real stream and I figured he just wanted those two hearts to mean something. But one time when Mom and I went to Upper Michigan I saw that there really was a Big Two-Hearted River."

"So he didn't make it up?"

"No. He did. I fished another river, called The Fox, while we were on that trip, and we stayed at a motel in a little town called Seney, which happens to be the name of the town Hemingway uses

[169]

in the story. And the stream seemed very similar to his descriptions, so when I got back to college I asked a Hemingway expert about it and he told me that The Fox was really the Big Two-Hearted and that Hemingway just liked the name." I was not prepared to explain what a "Hemingway expert" is so, since we were nearing the cut-off where we were to meet Sandy, I pointed ahead to where he was waiting.

"Did Hemingway catch a lot of fish in the story, Dad?"

"Nick did. Some big ones. On grasshoppers."

"Did you catch a lot?"

"Nope. I got bitten to shreds by the gnats and no-see-ums, and Mom did too, and I only caught two stocked brookies about six inches apiece, and your mother didn't go fishing with me again for seven years."

"Is Hemingway a better fisherman than you?"

But I had stopped the car by then and we both got out before I had to answer. Sandy was already in vest, Totes, and Montana felt hat.

We all walked down the stream, which was somewhat low but off-color, and Sandy tried a spot about a quarter of a mile upstream while I set up my Thomas slowly, knotted on a #14 Badger Variant and carefully ran the bottom three feet of leader through my mouth several times so it would sink easily. Sandy cast beautifully with his Payne, but took nothing. Nothing was moving on the surface.

Then, talking of old Jim Payne, who had recently died—one of the last of the master rod-makers—we headed far upstream to a spot where I knew the water was low, pocketed, and, since it ran over pebble and rock beds, probably clearer than this mud-bottomed section.

In the clearer water, Sandy quickly took a firm nine-inch brown from a pleasant pocket where the stream squeezed through a tight little drop and worked against and under the far bank. He beached it with care, carried it belly down in the cupped palms of his hands to another pocket some five yards across the stream, and there set it free. Then he returned, flicked his line deftly across stream several times, changed to a #18 Cahill, and cast again. I saw his rod arch up sharply: a good fish.

A few moments later, after losing it in the swift current, he headed upstream and was soon out of sight around the bend.

Paul had watched Sandy attentively and asked: "Do you think I can do that, Dad?"

"Next year, Son, you can start fly-fishing. Perhaps if I get a Pezon et Michel, you can have this little Thomas. Sandy gave it to me, to learn fly-fishing—and someday soon you can learn on it, too."

"Looks pretty hard, Dad."

We stood together and I cast the variant up into a riffle. It floated briskly for a foot or two, then disappeared in quick swirl. I struck lightly and felt a weight as the fish burrowed up into the current. It was a small brown and we soon beached it, released the hook carefully, and sent it back.

A few moments later Paul took a nice twelve-incher from the hole Sandy had been fishing, and then another from a fast run somewhat down-stream. We returned them both, though I noticed Paul's reluctance.

Soon Sandy came back, reported having taken four decent browns and released them, and then the three of us began to head back through the autumn fields.

Paul mentioned the returned trout several times, and I told him that they would be there and three or four inches larger in the spring. "That's good to know," I added.

"But Grandma won't believe we caught any," he said.

[172]

"Certainly she will. So will Mom."

"They won't," he insisted, shaking his head. "They never believe you."

"There," said Sandy, "is one of the principal sources of big kills: pride."

It was about five when we got back to the main portion of the river. I was a bit tired and half wanted to head home; Sandy, whose summer home was nearby, said he was ready to go.

I could do either. It had been a pleasant few hours and I could leave or not leave: we had all but rolled up the day and the season and put them into their case.

But Paul wanted to stay a bit longer, so we said good-bye to Sandy and headed for a long deep run I knew that sometimes held big fish in the early spring and late season. I'd always suspected it was a spawning hole.

The water was unpromising: fairly brownish, opaque, filled with floating leaves, slow and heavy. We caught nothing for five or ten minutes as we worked our way upstream together. The sun had dropped low and we were in a little valley which had grown quite chilly. Then I had a strike and handed the rod to Paul. It was only a rock bass. A few feet further upstream I hooked another, a scrappy smallmouth that leaped twice before coming to net. Then we took another rock bass, and then a sunfish.

We had turned the bend by now and I could see the head of the run, which began with only a few inches of water. There was an attractive pocket across and upstream about forty feet and I cast to it. A fish struck as soon as the fly touched the water and I had a good fish on; Paul fought him and we soon netted a fine ten-inch brown, which we decided to keep.

In the next half hour, standing there together in the autumn stream, in the darkening valley, we took about fourteen trout. Each cast brought a strike—almost the moment the fly touched the water. Paul took as many on his spinning rod and several times we were hooked up together, chattering to each other as we brought them in. We kept several and later their stomachs showed they were indeed spawners and I was sorry we had killed them: one had a long strip of milt and the other a pocket of roe. There must have been twenty or thirty trout schooled up in that short shallow run. I had not known they would strike so fiercely at this time. So quick, and emphatic were the rises that I swear they would have taken cigarette butts or tin foil or buttons had I cast them in.

It had been an exciting time. Paul was glad to have a few fish to take home and we were soon heading back through the fields—immensely pleased with ourselves, chattering away, a bit cold.

Just before we left the river to head up the hill to the car, I noticed that four or five trout were rising steadily in one of the most prominent pools. Since my rod was still rigged, I began to cast for them, but eight or ten casts brought not one rise.

"Ça va," I said to Paul. "That's the best way to end the season: seeing that trout aren't so silly after all."

He agreed. "I liked catching all those trout back there, Dad. I mean it was great. But that was really too easy, wasn't it?"

We unhinged our equipment carefully, packed it away, and were soon in the car heading home.

"Tell me some fishing stories, Dad," Paul said. So I told him one about a freckled boy who caught his first trout on a bare carlisle hook, hanging over a broken-down wooden bridge far back in the woods, and another about a cold Opening Day when a boy had caught four smallmouth bass and thought they were green perch, and a warden had come along, and he had taken the bass off the stringer and watched them revive; and another about a wild young man I once fished with who went after slashing trout in the moonlight with his bare hands; and another about a sweet endless trip to the Beaverkill, Mecca, with two good friends, and how one had mystified me with his spectacular skills.

And I watched my son's eyes glisten in the darkened car that we would soon have to sell, and tried to glance at the sunset to my right that he was pointing to: I only caught a few flashes of the salmon-flecked and streaked sky and a huge cloud formation now turned crimson and the streaks behind the foothills that Paul said were like the fingers of God patting the earth good night. And I thought of the withered yet upright corn stalks and the ghosts of dandelions and the late-blooming dandelions and the thistle with its purple mingled with gray, and the thin oblong yellow willow leaves coating the bottom of the stream.

"Frank Mele says," I told Paul, without turning from the dark road ahead of me, "that the Battenkill was terrific this year. He says that in certain riffles at dusk it's a Saturnalia, with the chop and slurp of rising trout surging in your ears.

They're hard though, those Battenkill browns. Takes a lot of skill to get many of those. Maybe we can fish it next year. Frank says that in the mornings the pools are tranquil, pure, evocative. And there are big trout there, Paul, some of them up to three pounds, I'll bet. Shall we try it, you and I, with fly rods, next spring? Paul?"

But the boy was asleep.

I took a deep breath, smiled, and in the speeding car said good-bye to the year, to the fields and streams that like a loon's call echoed through my very veins.